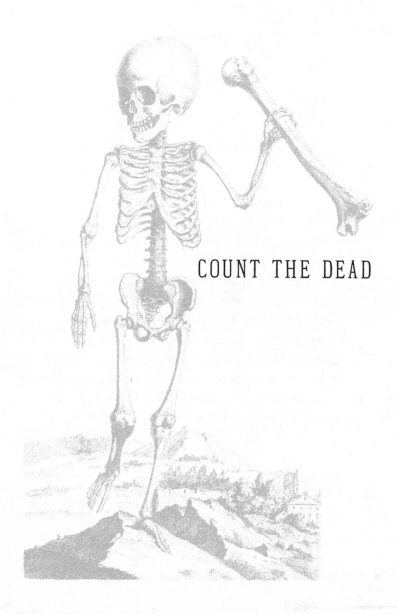

COUNT THE DEAD

THE STEVEN AND JANICE BROSE
LECTURES IN THE CIVIL WAR ERA

*Rachel Shelden, editor*
*William A. Blair, founding editor*

The Steven and Janice Brose Lectures in the Civil War
Era are published by the University of North Carolina
Press in association with the George and Ann Richards
Civil War Era Center at Penn State University. The
series features books based on public lectures by a
distinguished scholar, delivered over a three-day period
each fall, as well as edited volumes developed from
public symposia. These books chart new directions
for research in the field and offer scholars and general
readers fresh perspectives on the Civil War era.

# COUNT THE DEAD

## CORONERS, QUANTS, AND THE BIRTH OF DEATH AS WE KNOW IT

### STEPHEN BERRY

THE UNIVERSITY OF NORTH CAROLINA PRESS

*Chapel Hill*

This book was published with the assistance of the George and Ann Richards Civil War Era Center at Penn State University.

Designed by Jamison Cockerham
Set in Arno, Scala Sans, Blaisdell, and Rudyard
by Westchester Publishing Services

Cover illustration: Photo by Alexander Gardner, *Bodies of Confederate Artillerymen near Dunker Church*, 1862 (courtesy of Library of Congress Prints and Photographs Division, LC-DIG-ppmsca-32887).

Manufactured in the United States of America

The University of North Carolina Press has been a member of the Green Press Initiative since 2003.

LIBRARY OF CONGRESS CATALOGING-IN-PUBLICATION DATA
Names: Berry, Stephen William, author.
Title: Count the dead : coroners, quants, and the birth of death as we know it / Stephen William Berry.
Other titles: Steven and Janice Brose lectures in the Civil War era.
Description: Chapel Hill : University of North Carolina Press, 2022. | Series: Steven and Janice Brose lectures in the Civil War era | Includes bibliographical references and index.
Identifiers: LCCN 2021049359 | ISBN 9781469667515 (cloth ; alk. paper) | ISBN 9781469667522 (paperback ; alk. paper) | ISBN 9781469667539 (ebook)
Subjects: LCSH: Mortality—United States. | Registers of births, etc.—United States—History. | Public health—United States—History. | United States—Statistics, Vital—History—19th century. | United States—Statistics, Vital—History—20th century. | United States—Statistics, Vital—Social aspects. | United States—Statistical services—History.
Classification: LCC HA38.A1 B47 2022
LC record available at https://lccn.loc.gov/2021049359

# CONTENTS

# ILLUSTRATIONS & GRAPH

*Illustrations*

*Graph*

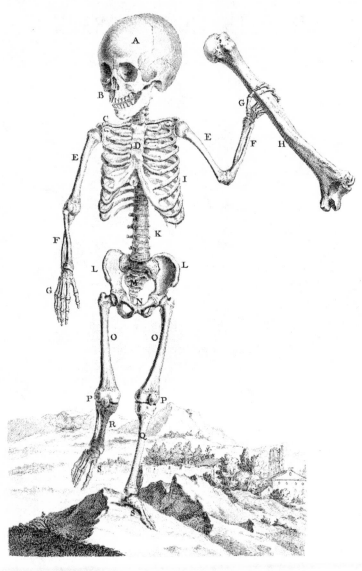

Plate from William Cheselden's *Osteographia* (1733), the first complete description, with illustrations, of human skeletal anatomy. William Cheselden, *Osteographia, or The Anatomy of the Bones* (London, 1733).

# PREFACE

# EVERY BODY MATTERS

*The only completely consistent people are the dead.*

ALDOUS HUXLEY

This is a book about death and data or, more specifically, about the dead as data. The dead and the formerly living are not the same. The formerly living built the Parthenon and the Brooklyn Bridge; we admire their work in the Louvre and in libraries. The formerly living also made brutal wars and ghastly decisions we are still struggling to live down. Revered or reviled, however, the formerly living have always counted because we still talk about them. Loved or hated, they built our world.

This is a book about a group that did not count for a very long time—the actual dead—the great ghostly horde who made their mark not in their living but in their collective dying, producing patterns of mortality that proved critical to the systematization of public health, casualty reporting, and human rights, the subjects of this book's three chapters.

Quantification has a long history. Forty thousand years ago, prehistoric humans invented the tally count, etching hash marks on sticks, like notches on a gun, to represent a count. The development of symbols for numbers took several more millennia, as did base systems and the concept of positional value (digits—named for our fingers—which had for eons done most of the counting). The Sumerians developed a sexagesimal system (base 60) because it was the smallest number divisible by every number from one to six, which may be why we still live our lives in sixty-minute hours. The Maya preferred a vigesimal system (base 20), with a shell denoting zero.[1]

Each of these developments represented a critical breakthrough in quantification, and yet with each new advance, no one counted the dead. The tally sticks that survive are devoted to sheep and seasons and debts. In 1834, the British Parliament immolated the willow tally sticks that had for ten generations represented the entire accounting system of the Exchequer. The ensuing fire burned Parliament to the ground.[2] "In our practical, money-making country," said one census superintendent glumly in 1850, we run "after those numbers which relate to the fluctuations of stocks, the valuation of exports and imports, the rates of taxation and the results in agriculture and manufactures, internal improvements and general commerce. [But] the life of man is of less importance than his larder and his cloth." (Machiavelli had said the same: "For men sooner forget the death of their father than the loss of their patrimony.")[3]

Even as the formerly living were honored with pyramids and burial ships—even as vast populations chased precise tonnages and times—no one saw the dead as a resource that could be collectivized and quantified and put to living work. In the second book of Samuel, King David was divinely punished for daring to order a census. Facing a war, he wanted to know whether he or his enemies had more fighting men. His determination to "number Israel," however, was seen as an unpardonable act of hubris. To atone, David was forced to choose the least of three evils: a pestilence that killed seventy thousand of his subjects. The message was clear: death should be left to the Almighty.

And so it went for ten thousand years, death doing its work in the dark. For eons we were a statistically rudderless species, surrendering ourselves up to providential (mis)fortune. And then, relatively recently, we counted the dead—not just some of them sometimes but most of them always—and the consequences were astounding. The resulting data helped double global human life expectancy and transform death itself. At the beginning of the nineteenth century, we died in our living rooms, tended by family members who quietly planted us in the ground. By the end of the century, we died later and more grudgingly, more often in hospitals, more often narcotized, enumerated postmortem and deployed in a variety of datafied forms.[4] "While nothing is more uncertain than a single life," said the early actuary Elizur Wright, "nothing is more certain than the average duration of a thousand lives." In one of the greatest achievements of humankind, we had disciplined death itself.[5]

The global doubling of human life expectancy between 1850 and 1950 is one of the most important things that has ever happened. Every technological breakthrough of the last century, every rise in every nation's gross domestic product, was made possible in part by the fact that we routinely live longer, less desperate lives. (Less optimistically, every burden that our planet now bears is a consequence of our sudden gain as a species. The environmental alarm bells ringing everywhere—insectageddons, septic oceans, and collapsing ecosystems—can all be traced to the dramatic rise in the number of people on the planet.)[6]

Historians rarely talk about this demographic sea change—this planetary adjustment to our abruptly long lives—and when they do, they tell a story of heroic medical breakthroughs: Edward Jenner develops the smallpox vaccine in 1796; quinine becomes broadly prescribed in the West by the 1850s; John Snow strikes a blow for germ theory in 1854; Joseph Lister publishes "An Address on the Antiseptic System of Treatment in Surgery" in

1868; Patrick Manson proves the "mosquito theory of malaria" in 1897; Alexander Fleming discovers penicillin in 1928.

This book does not deny the importance of these medical developments but rather seeks to highlight the deeper epistemological breakthrough that made them possible: datafying the dead.

As human beings, we have always been the canaries in our own coal mine. If you want to measure the relative health and happiness of any society, in any epoch, you'll find your best metric at the morgue. This may seem counterintuitive. When we say someone is "history," we mean they no longer matter. When we say someone is "dead" to us, we mean they no longer count. The problem is, they still do—or, at least, they still can. This book does not claim that the development of death records was sufficient in itself to produce revolutionary change, only that it was necessary. Human beings have always struggled to see at scale. What is right in front of us dominates our view; what is remote from us seems alien and unconnected. The death of a loved one is immediate, the death of a stranger less so. When a quarter million people die in a tsunami, it seems tragic, incomprehensible, and remote—an act of God. And yet we are all connected, as we have always been. To see at scale—to predict, adjust, and find the true meaning of our collective passing—we needed a new system of knowledge, a determination to count everything and everyone, including and especially the dead.

Statistics are central to how a state sees. The words are etymologically related for a reason. A state that can see can do good or bad things. The most chilling scenes in *Schindler's List* are not the random killings by Amon Göth but the stomach-churning sense that the Nazi state has committed itself to the modernization of murder. Desks await trains (that run on time), pencils are sharpened, the paperwork is ready. And yet to fight back, Schindler made a list of his own, because data is power.[7]

Michel Foucault, the philosopher-king of modern state history, dedicated the whole of his philosophy to the "art of not being . . . governed." He had every reason to resent state author-ity. As both a gay man and a committed revolutionary, Foucault knew the state primarily as a compeller of conformity. For him, the "dramatic expansion in the scope of government," including and especially the "increase in the number and size of the gov-ernmental calculation mechanisms," were all deplorable develop-ments. The more a state saw, the more it meddled, policed, and invaded.[8]

Toward the end of his life, however, Foucault began to soften. The radical revolutions of the 1960s had not only been defeated but self-defeated. Meanwhile, the welfare state had begun to (occasionally) take seriously its obligation to promote the great-est good for the greatest number. Dying of AIDS in 1984, Fou-cault left it to his principle student, François Ewald, to make the argument that the modern welfare state was, yes, "repressive and disciplinary" but also "open and playable."[9]

Open and playable, the modern state has done terrible and amazing things. We've learned to kill at an industrial scale, fire-bombing Hamburg and Tokyo; we've also parachuted into war-torn regions to eradicate smallpox. The point of this book is simple: if you want to measure how a state is actually doing, don't watch the news, watch the morgues. In 1991, the governing body of the Soviet Union voted itself out of existence after a popular referendum (the first in Soviet history) revealed massive sup-port for dissolution. By the end of the year, ten Soviet republics had declared their independence, and military units had com-pleted the demolition of the Berlin Wall. For Americans it all seemed a complete victory for democracy, humanity, and the self-determination of peoples. But all change has hidden human costs. As the privatization of the Russian economy concentrated power and wealth among a handful of oligarchs, the common people got sadder and the morgues got busier. Life expectancy of Russian men dropped to fifty-eight. Suicide rates rocketed upward—by 60 percent in Russia, 80 percent in Lithuania, and

95 percent in Latvia. People were dying of what we now call "deaths of despair"—alcoholism, drug abuse, and self-destructive behavior. "What we are arguing," said Omar Noman, coauthor of the definitive report on Russia's public health, "is that the [region's] transition to market economies is the biggest . . . killer we have seen in the 20th century, if you take out famines and wars. The sudden shock [of privatization] . . . has effectively meant that five million lives have been lost."[10]

As I write this preface, life expectancy in the United States has fallen for three years in a row, independent of COVID-19, which has obviously made everything worse. It's a steady reversal not seen in our country since 1918. In the past two decades, deaths of despair have risen dramatically, claiming hundreds of thousands of Americans each year, and the numbers are accelerating. Like bees, we are experiencing a sort of "colony collapse." *Count the Dead* takes us back to the moment when Americans first began to see that good data could be deployed to create better health outcomes for everyone. The central argument is simple: massive improvements in life expectancy and life quality came when we counted the dead and made them count. "Count," then, has dual meanings. Our obligation as a species is at once numerical and moral. Without a numerical count, we can't see at scale. Without a moral count, we create a record without a reckoning.[11]

 Chapter 1, "The Birth of Death as We Know It," chronicles the earliest American effort to generate a national death record—the mortality census of 1850. Prior to this first-ever survey of American public health, attempts to enumerate and classify the dead were deeply flawed and feebly executed. Conscientious priests kept records of all the weddings, baptisms, and last rites among their flock, only to be succeeded by rectors less persnickety. City registrars documented terrible epidemics and published "bills of mortality" in broadsides and newspapers, only to die in the next epidemic or get ousted in the next election. Until the nineteenth century, if you were the wrong race or religion, you generally didn't "count" among the dead. And even if you technically "counted," there was nothing technical about the count. Beginning with the 1850 mortality census, breakthroughs in nosology (disease classification), diagnostics, form design, calculating machines, vital statistics, and egalitarianism itself allowed us to count the dead and make them count—not some of them sometimes but all of them equally—enumerated en masse and put to work as data.[12]

The story of the global doubling of life expectancy between 1850 and 1950 is typically told as a series of heroic medical breakthroughs. Rarely is the story told as it is here, as a triumph of bureaucracy, a determination to count the dead—all of them—and figure out what we were actually dying of.

And once we did? We eradicated malaria in the South. We put niacin in our bread so we would stop dying of pellagra. We put fluoride in the water so we'd actually have teeth beyond the age of forty. And in one of the greatest achievements in human history, we slayed the dragon, eradicating smallpox—the greatest global killer of all humankind. For a short time, we did big things and could claim—at least sometimes, in some places—that the nine most magical words in the English language were "I'm from the government and I'm here to help."[13]

Chapter 2, "The Math of After," examines the evolution of casualty reporting and its impact on the American way of war. For most of American history, the federal government had a surprisingly laissez-faire attitude toward enumerating the dead and notifying the next of kin. On March 8, 1815, the *Daily Hampshire Gazette* (Northampton, Massachusetts) published a "Report of the Killed, Wounded and Missing of the Army under the command of Major Gen. Andrew Jackson" at the Battle of New Orleans. The dead included "1 lieutenant (M'Clellan) 1 serjeant, 1 corporal [and] 4 privates." Such a report, if ever it came under their eyes, could only have upset the families who had (unnamed) sergeants, corporals, and privates in Jackson's command. And yet there was at the time no sense that the federal government had an obligation to issue dog tags, notify families, make arrangements for the return of corpses, or even keep a record of exactly who had died in its name.[14]

Today, the U.S. military has a highly regimented process for notifying the families of fallen soldiers. Within four hours of the confirmation of death, two CNOs (casualty notification officers) in Class A uniforms (full suit, tie, jacket, ribbons, and medals) arrive at the residence of the NOK (next of kin) between 0600 and 2200. After identifying themselves, they "convey the notification message . . . without reading or appearing to read it . . . : 'The Secretary of the Army has asked me to express his deep regret that your (relationship: son, Robert[,] or husband, Edward; etc.) (died/was killed in action) in (country/state) on (date). (State the circumstances provided by the Casualty Area Command.) The Secretary extends his deepest sympathy to you and your family in your tragic loss.'" If the CNO is asked to assist in delivering the message to children, they are instructed to kneel down in order "to speak with them at their physical level."[15]

But even as we counted the war dead, we didn't always make them count. World War I was the "war to end all wars." In its aftermath, the major war-making countries signed the Kellogg-Briand Pact, promising never again to use war to resolve "disputes or conflicts of whatever nature or of whatever origin they may be." Then those same countries fought World War II, killing an estimated eighty-five million people, or 3 percent of the planet. In the aftermath of that war, those same countries created the United Nations "to save succeeding generations from the scourge of war, which twice in our lifetime has brought untold sorrow to mankind."[16] And then those same countries fought wars all over the globe. Granting, entirely, that there are good wars and bad wars, it is inarguable that after every war we remind ourselves that we should be careful not to do that again too easily, and then we too easily do it again. A tiny part of what makes this purposeful forgetting possible is the way we process casualties. As this chapter argues, we have two options: we can confront our war dead as an "elision"—an equestrian statue in a park or an homage to surviving veterans in a Memorial Day speech—or we can confront them in their totality, as a list. The latter produces less war or, at least, better wars.

Chapter 3, "The Power of a Name," focuses on the social justice dimensions of counting the dead. There is a famous biblical passage that says that we will be judged by how we acted toward "the least of these [our] brothers and sisters" (Matthew 25:40). The dead are the least of us; they are expendable. Unless we believe in ghosts, which most of us don't, our power of the dead is absolute; we could dispose of them in mass graves or let them rot upon the ground, ignoring them altogether. And yet in ways we forget, our humanity, as it did from the Stone Age, depends on how we treat "the least of these [our] brothers and sisters."

For all of recorded time, we have not died equally. "Died from severe, unmerciful and inhuman treatment and wounds inflicted by her owner" . . . "died from the effects of being beaten with a shingle by his owner" . . . "died from the whipping given her by William Tuggle" . . . "died in the consequences of the severity of [a] whipping inflicted on her by George Halson." This litany of findings by coroners' inquisitions convened in the nineteenth-century American South could go on for pages, and having read those pages, I can say that the emotions wash over you in waves of oscillating rage and despair. The question that remains in the aftermath is what to do. Justice can never be done; the parties to these events are already dead.[17]

And yet there is some small justice in knowing the truth, some small justice in naming names and setting the record straight. In 1786, the enslaved woman Jeny was murdered by William Tuggle. In 1823, the enslaved woman Nelly was murdered by George Halson. There is no statute of limitations on murder; William Tuggle and George Halson are murderers forever, and it is the historian's obligation to count the dead and keep the record until there can be a reckoning.

## CONCLUSIONS

In struggling to erect a data regime that could combat disease, early death, bad wars, and social injustice, the men and women discussed in this book created a new civic ethic—a shared belief that early death was a conquerable, controllable, common enemy that could only be defeated together. In (half-consciously) creating that ethic, these men and women fell afoul of far more than aggrieved citizens taking potshots at the census takers. They faced angry politicians who couldn't see the point of appropriating funds, economic interests that knew and feared what the data might reveal, and industries that moved ahead and behind the data-collection efforts, hoping to monetize the findings.[18]

Even so, over the course of the nineteenth century, census marshals, casualty processors, vital statisticians, actuaries, registrars, social justice advocates, and historians all became better at giving us a true accounting of who was dying of what, where, when, and why. The resulting data revolutionized criminal justice, public health, the insurance industry, and the discipline of history itself. In counting the dead, and making them count, we dramatically improved the experience of life on earth. The dead may not live among us as ghosts, but their afterlives as historical data have made us who we are.

*Count the Dead* is dedicated to the simple proposition that we owe the dead debts we rarely acknowledge. The dead may be the least of us, but as *information*, they remade the world. As public health data, they doubled the length of our lives. As casualty reports, they beg us to confront the human cost of war. As aggrieved ghosts, they call on us to make amends—and then to rest easy.

This book is dedicated to them.

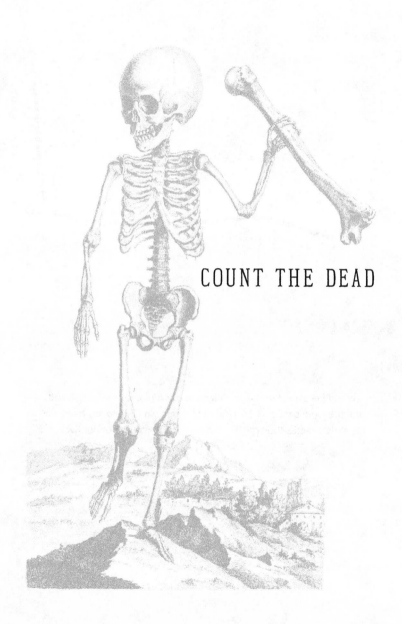

COUNT THE DEAD

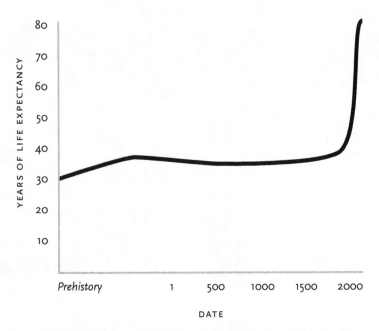

World life expectancy. For millennia, our biology, psychology, and culture were based on one mode of dying, which is to say relatively early. Practically yesterday, we doubled the length of our lives.
*Courtesy of author.*

# ONE

# THE BIRTH OF DEATH AS WE KNOW IT

*Statistics have "accomplished more in the last half century for the alleviation of misery, the prolongation of life, and the elevation of humanity, than all other agencies combined."*

JOSEPH C. G. KENNEDY, 1859

 OR most of recorded time, human life expectancy hovered around thirty. In the Western world, this number dipped slightly as societies industrialized and crowded into cities; then it rocketed upward, with the sharpest gains in the United States coming between 1890 and 1940. The global doubling of human life expectancy is arguably one of the most important things that has ever happened to our planet, on par with the asteroid that destroyed the dinosaurs and all that traveled in the train of the Columbian Exchange.[1]

There have always been humans who defied the law of averages. The average age at death of the first five American presidents

1

was eighty, a life expectancy the general populace would not reach until 2004. The Founding Fathers were unusual, however, and scholars have speculated that what selected them for greatness was not just their unusual brains but their unusual bodies. Certainly their longevity was not inherited by their children, who died at an average age of twenty-seven, then the national average.

What brought human life expectancy down before the twentieth century was high infant mortality rates and waves of infectious diseases that carried off old and young alike. The Antonine plague (A.D. 165) claimed ten million souls and arguably toppled the Roman Empire. "Weep not for me," Marcus Aurelius said on his deathbed. "Think rather of the pestilence and the deaths of so many others." This was nothing compared to the Plague of Justinian (A.D. 541–542), which claimed twenty-five million people—13 percent of the world. Even this was just a tune up for the Black Death, which swept away five times that number. Left in its wake, Francesco Petrarcha, "the Father of Humanism," was wracked with survivor's guilt. "What now, brother?" he wrote a colleague. "Our early hopes are buried with our friends. . . . Such final losses are irreparable, and the wounds inflicted by death can never be healed. There is but one source of consolation; we shall soon follow."[2]

And plague was just one of the microbial monsters we faced. At its height, smallpox carried off two million humans per year, holding particularly high revel among the Native Americans. "Where are the Pequot? Where are the Narragansett, the Mohican, the Pokanoket, and many other once powerful tribes of our people?" asked the Shawnee prophet Tecumseh despondently. "They have vanished . . . as snow before a summer sun." At its height in England, tuberculosis alone infected half the population and killed a quarter of them.[3]

Such numbers come home to us when we confront them on a smaller scale. We know the Brontës as the family that produced Emily, Anne, and Charlotte, authors respectively of *Wuthering*

*Heights, Agnes Grey,* and *Jane Eyre.* Between 1824 and 1855, the Brontës' cozy parsonage became the setting of a slow-motion murder mystery: six sick children cloistered away, writing of each other, to and for each other, as consumption claimed them all. In 1824, first-born Maria was described as "a girl of fine imagination and extraordinary talents"; her father claimed that he "could converse with [her] on any of the leading topics of the day as freely, and with as much pleasure, as with any adult." Maria went to school, came home with tuberculosis, and died at age eleven. Her younger sister, Elizabeth, attended the same school and died five weeks later, at age ten. Third-born Branwell, the lone boy of the family, lived far longer, though the sadness of his sisters' deaths ruined him before TB could. Writing morbid poems to Maria and drawing pictures of skeletons hovering over his bed, he drowned his depression in opium and alcohol, masking the symptoms of the galloping consumption that claimed him at age thirty-one. Remaindered and marooned were the most famous of the Brontës. Emily barely lived to see *Wuthering Heights* into print, succumbing to TB three months after Branwell, at age thirty. Weeks later, Anne wrote her "Last Lines," a prayer that God might spare her, coupled with the certainty that he wouldn't: "A dreadful darkness closes in / On my bewildered mind / Oh, let me suffer and not sin, / Be tortured, but resigned." "These lines written, the desk was closed, the pen laid aside— for ever," her sister Charlotte noted, and Anne was buried five months after Emily, at age twenty-nine. This left only Charlotte to wake each morning to see if Death was "standing at the gate," as Anne had put it. When it didn't come, she began to hope that she might escape her siblings' fate. She married and became pregnant before she was diagnosed with advanced tuberculosis. She died, along with her unborn baby, at a comparatively old age for a Brontë: thirty-eight.[4]

The Brontës were exceptionally unlucky, and there are demographers who argue that when you adjust for high infant mortality rates, most past peoples lived long enough into adulthood that they lived like us. Frankly, this is insane. First, it presumes that living into your forties is the same as living into your eighties. Second, it assumes that high infant mortality rates take no toll on parents. "This day, I feel doubly alone," wrote the novelist William Gilmore Simms in 1864 after burying nine of his thirteen children. "I have seen committed to the grave, year after year, children, wife & friends. The fiery circle of Fate is drawing rapidly around me."[5] Third, it assumes that if a majority of us make it to maturity we are unaffected by the large minority who do not. Racked by "spasmodic convulsions" that "almost rent asunder her very body," Virginia Poe endured an endless brutal rotten wasting putrescent deliquescing of the lungs—and nobody can say her death had no effect on her husband Edgar, who, in his grief, called the "death of a beautiful woman" the only subject worthy of a poem.[6]

Foreshortened life spans don't just mean that people live less; they live differently. The evanescence and unpredictability of life affects their culture. Amid the demographic devastation of the white plague, the Romantics transformed tuberculosis into a cultural style, political statement, and fashionable response because they were helpless to do anything else. Capitalism, industrialization, and international slavery became diseases. Tuberculosis became a cure for the disease of being—a portal and a metaphor and a way of seeing. "In 1823 and 1824, it was the fashion to suffer from the lungs," Alexandre Dumas noted in his memoirs. "Everybody was consumptive, poets especially; it was good form to spit blood after each emotion that was at all sensational, and to die before reaching the age of thirty."[7] Turning a disease into a fashion statement, the first bohemians inaugurated the Goth look. Death became them; our "heroin chic" was their "consumptive sublime." "For a poet to be over a certain weight," quipped one scholar, "was almost a crime against art."[8] "I look pale," Byron announced while looking in a mirror. "I should like to die of a consumption." "Why?" asked a friend. "Because the ladies would all say, 'Look at that poor Byron, how interesting he looks in dying!'"[9] Strolling his beloved woods, Thoreau noticed the maple leaves starting to turn, each with "a greenish centre and crimson border." "Decay and disease are often beautiful," he said, "like . . . the hectic glow of consumption." He died of TB at forty-eight. "For joy I could embrace the earth," he wrote in his journal, "I shall delight to be buried in it."[10]

War may be more storied and studied, but for thousands of years diseases and infections provided the gravest challenge to human life. For millennia, gangrene, sepsis, smallpox, influenza, cholera, yellow fever, tuberculosis, pellagra, and malaria were the great global killers. As late as 1915, only 3 percent of Americans made it to "the biblical age of three score and ten."[11]

And then, relatively overnight, we doubled the length of our lives. The story of this remarkable accomplishment is typically told as a series of heroic medical breakthroughs. Less celebrated is a more fundamental understanding: we owe our long lives to a triumph of bureaucracy and data.

 Bureaucracy gets a bad rap. Synonymous with red tape, sclerotic procedure, and death by committee, bureaucracy, like government itself, can seem grossly inefficient—experts and interests pulling in a thousand directions at once. And yet as the sum of our collective judgments, government bureaucracy can also be deliberative, careful, and relentless.

To understand the challenges a public health bureaucracy faced in the nineteenth century, let's take the example of New Orleans in 1853. Unlike most antebellum cities, New Orleans had a board of health, but it was ill equipped, ill informed, and disrespected. In May 1853, the board reported the first case of yellow fever in the city, but newspapers refused to cover the story, as the situation was not yet dire. A month later, the situation was so dire that newspapers refused to report the story lest panic dampen "the interests of trade." "Madam Rumor has given rise to the fancied existence of yellow fever in this city to a very great extent," reported the *Picayune*. "It is admitted that it has occurred in the city to the enormous extent of about four cases, a thing not unusual in any year past. But that it exists in a form or to an extent to produce alarm, except amongst old women, is most positively denied by all the most eminent physicians in the city."[12]

A month later, the city was in the grips of total panic, and the newspapers reversed course, blaming the board of health and city government for failing to do anything about streets that "looked and smelt epidemical," with gutters so filled with "carrion and carcasses and festering nastiness of every description" that they seemed to "exhale" "filthy compounds [and] abominable smells." When a local physician dared advance the "strange and absurd theory" that the gutter garbage was not the source of the scourge, he was denounced as "a fool who deserved pity, or a knave who deserved the severest punishment." And when a rare summer deluge washed out the gutters, the newspapers greeted it as "Providential interference." "Could we only calculate upon as much rain once or twice every week of the summer!" exclaimed the *Delta*. "The weather is the strangest ever known in the city," noted the *New Orleans Commercial Bulletin*. "It is regular April weather, almost in the middle of July!"[13]

The "strange" weather was the problem; the heavy summer rains fed the pools of standing water that served as breeding grounds for yellow fever's carrier: the female *Aedes aegypti* mosquito. A fifth of the city died, and the blame went nowhere it belonged. Racists blamed the city's "foreigners," meaning southern Europeans, for "bad hygiene." Political reformers blamed the city's grotesquely corrupt politicians. The corrupt politicians blamed the reformers for failing to pass infrastructure bills that would surely have helped (their own pocketbooks). And everyone blamed the only organization that had tried to make a difference: the board of health. "Will the proper officers please inform the public, who compose the 'Board of Health?'" the *Picayune* asked sarcastically. "Does such a body exist?" It might as well not have.[14]

To be effective, a public health system requires three things: an accurate conception of the problems, a capacity to implement real solutions, and the political will to act. In the early 1800s, the United States largely lacked all three. (Even the expectation that government should act in this sector would need to be invented.)[15]

At the level of the individual, we all die anecdotally. Watching a few of us go out of the world, American scientists and physicians flew blind, more likely to assume their own findings and confirm their own stereotypes. When Benjamin Rush, the leading medical man of his era, noticed that Philadelphians seemed to be living a little longer, he postulated that the declining use of wigs, the increased use of umbrellas (then a recent invention), or the introduction of round hats was responsible for the change. The only way to know that hats and wigs aren't killing people is to collect the data.[16]

As historian Patricia Cline Cohen has noted, the first half of the nineteenth century witnessed a dramatic expansion in quantification, numeracy, and data gathering in the United States. The reasons were manifold. The rise of a market economy required and rewarded precision; common schools made the mass of men mathematically literate, and the profit motive focused them on the bottom line. By the 1830s, American newspapers were awash in numbers: prices, tonnages, times. "Their minds [are] accustomed to definite calculations," Tocqueville said of Americans. This growth of numeracy had its less savory side. Herman Melville wrote *The Confidence Man* in this period, and Edgar Allan Poe wrote "Diddling Considered as One of the Exact Sciences." After a sojourn in the United States, Charles Dickens noted that

Americans' most "prominent feature" was a "love of 'smart' dealing, which gilds over many a swindle and gross breach of trust." But the rise of numeracy also offered a new data-driven foundation for dramatic improvements in sanitation and public health.[17]

Critical to the change was the evolution of a simple civic dictum: count the dead. In 1845, when pioneering statistician Lemuel Shattuck first began agitating the Massachusetts legislature for the adoption of a statewide death registration system, he was inspired in part by the wretched state of Boston's death records, then the best in the country. "It is much to be regretted," Shattuck concluded, "that our system of registration is such, that we cannot present, in any period of our history, an accurate account." Forty years later, U.S. surgeon general Joshua S. Billings could claim with the flatness of fact that it "is now . . . generally admitted that it is the duty of a State to protect its citizens against unnecessary disease and death." Billings had had a front-row seat to one of the greatest demographic revolutions in human history, and he gave the lion's share of the credit to the evolution of mortality statistics. Death registration, he said, had become, "as it were, the eyes of the State Board of Health, and without it the Board is like a blind man trying to put out a prairie fire."[18]

Between 1840 and 1880, quants like Shattuck and Billings began to extinguish the prairie fire that had burnt through mankind for millennia. They did it with data, and they did it on a government paycheck. To be sure, the story of the rough doubling of life expectancy depended equally on medical breakthroughs—antisepsis, vaccines, antibiotics—but the collection, analysis, and visual display of compelling information was critical to advancing sanitary science and compelling the public to act. "A board of health, or health officer, in this 'government of the people, by the people, for the people,'" Billings said, "can do good, effective, paying work so far, and only so far, as the people can see and understand that the work is needed, and worth doing and paying for."[19]

# LEMUEL SHATTUCK,
## TRANSCENDENTAL BUREAUCRAT

The fifth of six children, Lemuel Shattuck was born on a remote farm in Ashby, Massachusetts, in 1793. His father was a farmer and shoemaker with a strong work ethic and a stronger faith; the Bible, he said, was his one "need-ful" thing. Unfortunately, the Shattucks quickly developed "a tendency to that fearful disease which takes away the lives, and destroys the hopes of many New England families." Mother Betsey died of consumption when Shattuck was only four years old. Ten years later, Shattuck ran in tears to his sister's house to get help: their father "lay upon his back . . . in agonies," "his mouth, from the difficulty of breathing, open—his eyes shut—his heaving lungs pressed with phlegm, which rattled in his throat at every breath. . . . He tried to speak, but utterance was denied him [and] he lay in great distress during the whole night [until] morning came [when] a serene stillness reigned."[20]

Shattuck had barely recovered from his father's death when his youngest sister fell sick. In her case, the tuberculosis progressed rapidly—the so-called galloping consumption, in which chills, fever, rapid pulse, and labored breathing quickly ends in death by sepsis and exhaustion. She died a year after her father, at age twenty. By then, Shattuck realized that he would lose his older sister, too. She died of consumption in 1822, at the age of thirty.

It does not take a biographer's leap of logic to imagine that the sequential early deaths of his mother, father, and two favorite sisters had a lasting effect on the man who would go on to be the American pioneer of mortality statistics. Certainly Shattuck never said "I became interested in death data because of the demographic decimation of my family." What he *did* say was

Lemuel Shattuck.
*Courtesy of National Library of Medicine.*

that his sisters had died "just as they were maturing into woman-hood, and were about to take their stations as heads of families, and as useful members of society. Their career was arrested, and they were numbered with that great multitude of similar cases, in which Providence seems mysteriously to select the most meritorious, and those of the greatest promise."[21]

With little tying him to home, Shattuck moved to Concord, Massachusetts, to open a bookstore with his brother. There, by gradual degrees, he remade himself into the hub of an international community of readers, authors, and publishers debating the latest breakthroughs in history, philosophy, and science;

and there he first came across the article that would change his life: Edwin Chadwick's "Life Assurances—Diminution of Sickness and Mortality," published in 1828 in the *Westminster Review*. At the core of Chadwick's article was a careful comparison of the life tables that England's life insurance companies had used over time. In tabulating the data, Chadwick proved that human life expectancy *was* improving in England, and it was *especially* improving in those urban areas where increased sanitation, access to medical care, and sound city planning had begun to take hold. For years, Chadwick said, sanitary science had been "treated as a 'mere theory'" by the "practical men" who always had one reason or another to resist regulation and reform. Here, finally, was the proof that sanitation saved lives. Any man who now stood in the way of change was guilty of something close to murder.[22]

Chadwick's article was an exposé and a call to arms. Moving to Boston, Shattuck decided to see if he could re-create Chadwick's experiment in an American context using the city's bills of mortality (an annual death registry kept by the city registrar). Tabulating the numbers, Shattuck was astounded. The scandal Chadwick had exposed had been small *improvements* in life expectancy that were being covered up by legislatures and life insurance companies. What Shattuck discovered was sadder: life expectancy in Boston was declining. The city's Black population was being decimated, as were its children. "It is a melancholy fact," Shattuck said, that "nearly half of all deaths which have taken place in Boston during the last nine years, are of persons under 5 years of age; and the proportional mortality of this age has been increasing." As Boston had become more crowded, the city had become more lethal, and children were paying the price. Shattuck suspected that the culprit was poverty—bad air, bad jobs, bad water, bad diets, bad habits—but as he often said of himself in the plural: "We are not a theorist. We are a statist—a dealer in facts." Whatever his suspicions, he would need to find the proof.[23]

Here, however, Shattuck was stymied. The Boston records were so incomplete they could hardly be made to prove anything. A third of the causes of death were listed as undetermined or unknown. Many others were so vague as to be meaningless. Many entries were missing age, sex, race, profession. All were missing addresses. Worse still, Boston had one of the best death registration systems in the country. New York, Philadelphia, Baltimore, and New Orleans also had systems, but Shattuck (rightly) suspected that they were even worse, and these cities accounted for only 6 percent of the American population. Statistically speaking, Shattuck said, sanitary efforts in 94 percent of the country were like boats with snapped masts drifting rudderless and beset by fog in uncharted water.[24]

England had adopted a national death registration law in the aftermath of the cholera epidemic of 1832. (Shattuck had hailed it as "the most important sanitary measure ever adopted.") France, Prussia, Switzerland, Italy, and Scandinavia had all followed suit by 1840. Why was America so late to act? What, to be blunt, was America's problem?[25]

First, the United States was big, sprawling, and rural. Death registration worked best among dense populations stitched together by tight roads and tighter bureaucracy, and America had little of that infrastructure. In 1840, more than 17 million Americans were strewn across a countryside that measured almost 2 million square miles—a population density of fewer than 10 people per square mile. England had a slightly smaller population (13.6 million) crammed into a much smaller space (50,000 square miles) for a population density of 273. In America, it was difficult enough to take the census every ten years; how could registrars possibly record every death that occurred in every slapdash cowshed across the American frontier?[26]

This was not the only problem. Far more than any European power, the United States had a deeply federated system. States enacted laws that counties might ignore, and national systems of

The preceding table, (Table V,) being the first compiled from the printed bills of mortality, presents a general view of the number of deaths each year, from 1811 to 1839, distinguishing the males from the females. The still-born, having never lived, are excluded from the number of deaths in all correct bills of mortality, and are here placed in a separate column. The population at the different enumerations, and the estimated population for the intervening years, and the ratio which the deaths bear to the population, are given. The least mortality in one year was in 1827, being 939, one in 63, or 1.57 per cent., and the greatest in 1821, being 1,321, one in 35, or 2.85 per cent. The average annual deaths were 813, from 1811 to 1830—one in 47, or 2.09 per cent., 1147 from 1821 to 1830—one in 49, or 2.05 per cent., and 1,552 from 1831 to 1839—one in 46, or 2.14 per cent., showing a small increase in the force of mortality.

*Mortality of different Ages.*—The number of deaths varies very much in the different ages, being in some much greater than in others. We have presented in table VI the number who have died under 1, between 1 and 2, 2 and 5, 5 and 10, and at each subsequent decennial period of life. This has been done for the different sexes, and in the different periods of time—the 10 years, 1811 to 1820, and 1821 to 1830, and the 9 years, 1831 to 1839, that we might institute a comparison between the different periods, to ascertain whether the proportion of deaths was the same in each, and also for the whole 29 years. The greatest number of deaths in any one period mentioned, is under one year, in the period 1831 to 1839, being 2861. The next greatest is between 20 and 30 of the same period, being 1843. The least number is between 90 and 100.

TABLE VI, *showing the influences on the number of deaths in different ages, distinguishing the males from the females, in three different periods of time.*

| Age. | 1811—1820. | | | 1821—1830. | | | 1831—1839. | | | 1811—1839. | | |
|---|---|---|---|---|---|---|---|---|---|---|---|---|
| | Males | Females | Total. | ales | Females | Total | Males | Fem'ls | Total. | Males | Fem'ls | Total. |
| Under 1 | 765 | 610 | 1375 | 1129 | 833 | 1962 | 1596 | 1265 | 2861 | 3490 | 2708 | 6198 |
| 1 to 2 | 435 | 397 | 832 | 580 | 640 | 1220 | 848 | 933 | 1781 | 1863 | 1970 | 3833 |
| 2 to 5 | 267 | 224 | 491 | 438 | 365 | 793 | 849 | 749 | 1598 | 1544 | 1338 | 2882 |
| 5 to 10 | 151 | 133 | 284 | 233 | 173 | 406 | 344 | 275 | 619 | 728 | 581 | 1309 |
| 10 to 20 | 194 | 236 | 430 | 234 | 299 | 533 | 272 | 463 | 735 | 700 | 998 | 1698 |
| 20 to 30 | 548 | 585 | 1133 | 671 | 733 | 1404 | 871 | 972 | 1843 | 2090 | 2290 | 4380 |
| 30 to 40 | 509 | 471 | 980 | 750 | 642 | 1392 | 913 | 738 | 1651 | 2172 | 1851 | 4023 |
| 40 to 50 | 497 | 374 | 871 | 623 | 466 | 1089 | 651 | 505 | 1156 | 1771 | 1345 | 3116 |
| 50 to 60 | 300 | 260 | 560 | 389 | 331 | 720 | 456 | 365 | 821 | 1145 | 956 | 2101 |
| 60 to 70 | 201 | 255 | 456 | 233 | 287 | 520 | 303 | 343 | 646 | 737 | 885 | 1622 |
| 70 to 80 | 160 | 226 | 386 | 181 | 248 | 429 | 198 | 298 | 496 | 539 | 772 | 1311 |
| 80 to 90 | 74 | 119 | 193 | 80 | 137 | 226 | 85 | 140 | 225 | 248 | 396 | 644 |
| 90 to 100 | 5 | 24 | 29 | 11 | 26 | 37 | 15 | 36 | 51 | 31 | 86 | 117 |
| Sum | 4106 | 3914 | 8020 | 5551 | 5180 | 10731 | 7401 | 7082 | 14483 | 17058 | 16176 | 33234 |
| Unknown | 50 | 62 | 112 | 396 | 343 | 737 | 56 | 34 | 90 | 502 | 439 | 941 |
| Total | 4156 | 3976 | 8132 | 5947 | 5523 | 11470 | 7457 | 7116 | 14573 | 17560 | 16615 | 34175 |

any kind were rare. In a country that didn't have a national currency until 1862, how likely was it that it could pass and enforce a national death registration act? Where was the political will going to come from? What might such data say about slavery? What might it say about the relative healthfulness of competing cities? In any era, businesses don't like to be investigated any more than they like to be regulated, even and especially if our collective public health is about to be exposed.[27]

And then there was the simple matter of qualified manpower. In the period before civil service reform, positions that might technically require continuity and expertise were part of the patronage system. When one political party swept the other out of office, virtually every government job turned over. Forget the deep state; the nineteenth century was no "shallow" state. Take the case of Shattuck's New York City counterpart, John H. Griscom. Griscom had been appointed city inspector of New York in 1842, and he had immediately gone to work on a brilliant and devastating sanitary survey of the city's tenement buildings. By the end of the year, he had been sacked when the Whigs were beaten "horse, foot & raccoons" in the city elections and the Locofocos cleaned house. "My work is unfinished, scarcely begun," Griscom lamented to Shattuck, "but hungry politicians care but little for those things. . . . If I must go, the little good I may have done is likely to be lost." Griscom was right. It would be sixty years before New York City enacted meaningful tenement reform.[28]

Shattuck worried that even if by some miracle a national registration act could be passed and the offices staffed, what chance was there that Americans would comply? Skepticism of government intrusion was the birthright of every American. William Faulkner famously depicted the American male as a "married invincible bachelor without destination but only motion . . . scattering his inexhaustible seed in three hundred miles of dusky bellies." Such a characterization was flippant and grotesque but not entirely untrue. In a country where resentment of authority was rampant, where bastardy rates were high, where rape of the enslaved was endemic, where exploitative labor practices were the norm, white men generally wanted a government that sponsored profits and turned a blind eye to abuse—two sides of the same coin. As one newly installed death registrar for California described it in 1859, the state's foreign-born citizens were familiar with death registration and tended to comply in every particular. But the "Jo. Bowers' people"—by which he meant Faulkner's frontier types—were "deadly hostile" to any record that wasn't made on the ground in chalk before the rain came. "That a regulation so useful in its character [should] meet with [such] strenuous opposition," he said of his own death registration effort, "is a problem beyond my comprehension, and which I leave for others to solve."[29]

Data collection met resistance even among Shattuck's fellow intellectuals. In rejecting the excesses of industrialization—the rise of materialism and market capitalism—the Brahmins of the Romantic age sought their solace in folk wisdom, mysticism, intuition, art, poetry, untamed nature, and a general doctrine that the "government is best which governs least." This is a fine philosophy, but as Shattuck discovered, it doesn't leave much room for the public health bureaucrat. The Romantics had a natural skepticism of facts, figures, tables, bureaucratic systems, and solutions—all of which had helped create the Industrial Revolution in the first place, reducing men to machines, the enslaved to things, and ushering in a period when the "mass of men lead lives of quiet desperation." Mathematical figures, in the Romantic experience, knew everything of profits and nothing of justice. "Nothing comes to the book-shops but politics, travels, statistics, tabulation and engineering," complained Ralph Waldo Emerson. "To what purpose make more big books of these statistics?

There are already mountains of facts, if any one wants them. But people do not want them. They bring their [own] opinion into the world."[30]

To Shattuck, such thinking was ludicrous. Free thought and self-reliance are all well and good, but a man who evacuates his bowels in a bucket is not quite entitled to his own opinion as to whether he is dying of cholera, particularly when he plans to dump the bucket in the city water supply. "Numerical Tables constitute a species of literature, the least attractive, yet discovered," said one reviewer of Shattuck's work. "Whoso wisheth to do scientific penance, let him read 100 pages of his figures." What people failed to see was the humanity and inhumanity, the human possibilities and tragedies, Shattuck saw in his numbers. Shattuck presented himself as a tireless statist and "purveyor of facts"— the quintessential quant—but what drove him was the moral urgency that came from seeing preventable death all around him. Indeed, the moral blindness of his fellow Americans occasionally drove him to despondency. Where there was a dollar to be made, they were cunning as jackals; where there was a life to be saved, they were clodpated as mules. "Manufactures have been so far investigated," Shattuck lamented, "that the cost of every article—material, transportation, labor, wages, board, &c.—is clearly known. But what amount of life is sacrificed thereby we know not. . . . We ought to know how far our habits—the universal thirst for wealth in America, the reckless speculations of some, the hap-hazard mode of living and disregard to health of others, the luxury and extravagance of certain classes . . . check the progress of the population."[31]

Logistically, politically, and culturally, Shattuck knew a national registration scheme faced a steep uphill climb. Shattuck was nothing if not an indefatigable grind, however. In reviewing one of his books, the *North American Review* captured the whole of the man in a sideways compliment: "Nothing but inveterate industry and unshrinking perseverance, nothing but the professional enthusiasm by which they are sustained could have enabled our annalist to undertake to undergo the years of dismal drudgery of which his book bears evidence on every page."[32]

Shattuck's first move was to professionalize statistics and improve America's technocratic infrastructure. In 1839 he founded the American Statistical Association (the second oldest professional association in the United States, after the Massachusetts Medical Society). Simultaneously, he began work on the wretched state of the data itself, lobbying the Massachusetts state legislature to create and then improve the nation's first statewide death registration system. His most far-reaching accomplishment, however, was redesigning the American census, one of the more underappreciated data revolutions in the history of the country.[33]

 The first-ever census of the United States, taken in 1790, is a list of (mostly) white men's names—heads of households with their dependents and slaves enumerated and unnamed beneath them. This simple fact—the data structure of the census—reveals something critical about how the American government understood its own country. The word *husband* comes from the Old Norse *hús* (house) coupled to *bóndi* (tiller of the soil). In its very etymology, the husband is the center of the house, and the house is the center of economic activity. The etymology of *wife* is very different—it simply means "woman." These etymologies lend context to the term *household*, which encompassed a husband, a wife, and the children, slaves, and servants that a husband's *hús* protected (and exploited). The word *hold*, like the word *keep*, implied a place of physical protection, the penumbra of safety around an (ostensibly) powerful male. *Hold* had other, equally relevant meanings, however: "to have or keep in the hand; keep fast; grasp; to keep in a specified state or relation." In 1790 (and through 1840), the state treated the household as the irreducible data unit of American life; it functioned as the atom before the discovery of subatomic particles.

What Shattuck proposed to do was to split the atom: the census should record the names and personal statistics of every man, woman, and child in America; everyone should get a line. State bureaucracy can care about people for right and wrong reasons. Hitler's Germany would later be ruthlessly precise about who was who. But Shattuck's simple data revolution had profound implications for everything from public health to social equality in the United States. Being equal *as data* is not sufficient to make us equal *as people*, but it was, as we'll see, a necessary precondition.[34]

Shattuck tested his new data conception on Boston first. In his resulting *Census of Boston* (1845), the city council inserted a little preface: here is a "vehicle not only of general information," they noted, but a book "that introduces the brotherhood of man to a more intimate acquaintance with one another, and enables the citizens of countries however remote, to contribute something essentially beneficial to others of the human family." Shattuck must have been pleased to be finally understood. He was just as much a transcendentalist as Emerson, as much a believer in divine human potential. He just happened to believe that our potential could never be reached until someone paid attention to the numbers.[35]

## JOSEPH C. G. KENNEDY AND THE REFORMATION OF THE CENSUS

In 1849, when Congress typically would have debated and authorized the upcoming census, House members were busy trading body blows (sometimes literally) over the future of slavery in the territories. "We dream of negroes, hear nothing else by the wayside or in the House [or] at our meals," complained one vitriolic legislator. With little oxygen left for anything else, congressmen responded typically and on the last day of the session authorized the formation of a board to deal with the census, then fled the Capitol.[36]

When they returned in 1850, many were surprised (and some were appalled) by how much had been achieved. In their absence, President Zachary Taylor had appointed Pennsylvanian Joseph C. G. Kennedy to chair the U.S. Census Board. A political appointee with few obvious qualifications, Kennedy knew enough to call Lemuel Shattuck. Together they formulated a census questionnaire more ambitious than any seen before, a questionnaire that followed Shattuck's Massachusetts model of gathering names and details on every man, woman, and child in America. Specifically: Schedule 1 would tabulate the name, address, age, sex, color, occupation, place of birth, and marital status of every free American, asking them whether they had attended school within the year; whether they were deaf, dumb, blind, insane, idiotic, or a pauper; and whether they owned any real estate and, if so, how much. Schedule 2 would document each slave's name, age, sex, color, and place of birth, along with whether they were deaf, dumb, blind, insane, idiotic, or a fugitive, and, in the case of women, how many children they had borne in which state and whether those children were now living or dead. Schedule 3 would ask a separate battery of questions about anyone who had died on the property in the preceding year. Schedules 4 and 5 would focus on agriculture and manufacturing, and Schedule 6 would seek to pull together social statistics about taxes, schools, newspapers, pauperism, crime, wages, religion, and libraries. Confident in his work, sure of his authority, and worried about his deadlines (the census was supposed to be taken over a one-month period in the summer), Kennedy sent the new forms to the printer and sat back to await his much-deserved praise.

Kennedy had achieved such a dramatic expansion of the census that the reconvened legislators had a difficult time gutting it all, although they certainly did their best. As might be guessed, Schedule 2 drew the lion's share of the scrutiny. In previous censuses, the enslaved population had been treated as property attached to the household. A male head of house, for instance, might be listed as having four male slaves between the ages of ten and twenty, three female slaves between the ages of forty and fifty, and two slave children under the age of ten. Kennedy's questionnaire intended to *name* the enslaved and then ask about their children and their families. Grilled by Congress, Kennedy claimed that the reforms were designed only to ensure greater accuracy; a census marshal would be less prone to error, he suggested, if he could use the slaves' names as a check against over- or undercounting. Certainly there were bound to be fewer Celias on a plantation than there were girls between ten and twenty. Congressmen instantly seized on the radical implications of the data Kennedy sought to gather, however. Senator Andrew Butler of South Carolina demanded that no slave names should be recorded, a motion that quickly passed. Senator William King of Alabama then demanded that no data should be gathered on where the enslaved had been born, a motion that also passed. Such data would be invaluable today; African Americans tracing their ancestry would have ancestors' names to go by and, given a sense of the (forced) movements of the enslaved, historians would have a much better sense of the scale, scope, and timing of the Second Middle Passage—the sale of a million men, women, and children down the river to the Cotton Kingdom.[37]

Whatever they told themselves about the "positive good" of slavery, southern congressmen seemed perfectly unwilling to face what Kennedy's statistics might reveal. Most dramatically, they knew the proposed question about the parentage of enslaved children might draw census marshals into conversations about whose mulatto children were whose. Congressman King tried to treat it all as a joke. There was no point in asking such questions, he said, because in his experience, "the [slave] woman herself, in nine out of ten cases, when she has had ten or fifteen children, does not know how many she has actually had." This amused most of his Senate colleagues, but New York senator William Seward did not get the joke. "There is no woman," he said, "with great deference to the Senator from Alabama, who can have forgotten the number of children that she has borne." Seward then proposed adding *another* question to Schedule 2: "I wish to know also what is the extent of the education or of instruction that prevails [among the enslaved], so as to ascertain whether they are advancing toward that better condition which constitutes, the only excuse, as I understand, that we have for holding them." As Seward was being pilloried for his inflammatory remarks, Senator Underwood of Kentucky attempted to pacify things by noting that the resulting infant mortality data might be useful for the burgeoning southern business of slave life insurance. Kennedy's Schedule 2 was dead on arrival, however. Gutted by Congress, he was ordered to cancel his contract with the printer and prepare new forms.[38]

What had escaped Congressional attention in all the hubbub, however, was Schedule 3. And thus was born the 1850 mortality census, the first-ever federal public health survey in the history of the United States—the strange stepchild of the precise attention of statisticians and the lax oversight of Congress.

To be sure, the resulting mortality survey was a total mess. According to official instructions, all census agents were ordered to complete the work of Schedules 1 (population) and 2 (the neutered slave schedule) and then ask if any member of the household had died during the previous year—specifically between the dates of June 1, 1849, and May 31, 1850. If so, the agent was to ask the name, age, sex, race, occupation, status (free or slave), marital status, and place of birth of the deceased as well as the cause of death, season of death, and duration of the illness, if applicable.

There are myriad problems with this approach. First, one can imagine that many census marshals were, by Schedule 3, chafing to move on to the next household and not particularly keen to discuss the health histories of the recently deceased with potentially still-grieving family members. The underclass of the antebellum backwoods had little affection for strangers and liked strangers asking questions even less. To them, the census takers were the vanguard of the taxmen. "We escaped without any drubbings," said one marshal of his experience, but "we came unpleasantly near catching a dozen."[39]

Even if census agents were up to the task of cross-questioning the pugnacious hoi polloi, they faced family members with innumerable reasons to withhold information. Who would answer the door to a government employee and confess to a murder? What farmer of the period would tell a perfect stranger that his unwed daughter had died on the birthing couch or that one of his slaves had died from a whipping or an amputation meant as punishment? Given such circumstances, underreporting on the mortality census was certainly significant and perhaps even massive.

Then there was the opposite problem: more than a few Americans felt perfectly comfortable sharing intimate (and erroneous) details with strangers; hundreds of unfortunates were recorded as having died of menstruation, masturbation, herpes, and other unlikely scenarios. This raises a third problem with the mortality census: it had tasked people not remotely versed in medicine to pronounce a cause of death. The Census Office had anticipated this problem, but by the time it began dealing with it, Joseph Kennedy had been sacked as census superintendent.

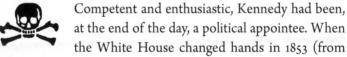 Competent and enthusiastic, Kennedy had been, at the end of the day, a political appointee. When the White House changed hands in 1853 (from Whig Zachary Taylor to Democrat Franklin Pierce), it was time for government employees to be patronized and punished. Given the Democrats' strong base in the South, the choice of James

D. B. De Bow as the new census superintendent made a good deal of sense. Living in New Orleans, De Bow was famous across the south as the editor and writer of *De Bow's Review*. "Just as a homeowner today might subscribe to a magazine like *This Old House*," Ta-Nehisi Coates has written, "slaveholders had journals such as *De Bow's Review*, which recommended the best practices for wringing profits from slaves." Making the case for reparations, Coates was exaggerating for effect, but not much. De Bow was a sophisticated statistician and demographer, however, well versed in tabulating data. In this sense, he was better qualified than Kennedy, and in 1853 he relocated to Washington to begin preparing the 1850 census for publication.[40]

While Kennedy had left the office in good shape, De Bow felt compelled to put his stamp on the place, reorganizing staff and workflows. By the time he got around to the headaches inherent in the mortality data, he was well behind schedule and thoroughly worn down. Hunched over tiny type for long hours over several months, he seemed almost wistful in introducing America to its first federal health survey:

> It was the remark of a physician, now no more, founded
> on severe experience, that the lawyer who saved the
> property of his client was always quicker, better and
> more cheerfully paid than the doctor who saved his life.
> Steamboat and railroad companies understand this well
> enough, for whilst they must pay heavily for destroying
> a bundle of merchandise, in human life they can and
> do wanton at pleasure. Such being the case, it is not
> singular that investigations having for their object sanitary
> improvement are pursued slower and later in all countries
> than those which relate to property. They meet with
> greater impediments and their results are least consulted
> or credited. Man is the same in all ages, and this fact meets
> us in all.[41]

De Bow struck a similarly ambivalent tone throughout the volume. He had no illusions, he admitted, about the quality or completeness of the data. He guessed that "in the Union at large at least one-fourth of the whole number of deaths have not been reported at all." (He was right; worse still, the major cause of death of the three-fourths that were collected was "Unknown.") De Bow was sure that the rural population had been better counted than the urban and that the older states were better enumerated than the newer. The result was a set of data that was probably worthless for making regional or state comparisons. Did fewer people die in Mississippi, or did Mississippi do a poorer job recording deaths? Finally, De Bow worried about the self-reported nature of the data. Among the educated, he said, the claimed causes of death "may be considered sufficiently near the truth for popular purposes, though falling far short of the precision necessary in skillful scientific calculations." But among the masses, "vagueness and inaccuracy may naturally be expected, even where the parties are disposed to speak the truth and make the best effort to do so."[42]

Given all the problems—the flawed design of the survey, the biases and lackluster performance of the census marshals, the unequal and cantankerous participation of the respondents—it is unsurprising that today's demographers have generally eschewed the first mortality census as a set of "bad data" they would not touch with a ten-foot slide rule. To the historian, however, no data are inherently bad. All data are evidence of *something*; all data tell a story, even if it isn't the story the data were collected to reveal. While the self-reported nature of the mortality census makes the resulting data bad if you are interested in an accurate set of medical diagnoses, it is good if you are interested in, say, vernacular death—what common people thought they were dying of. If a woman thought her son died of masturbation, surely it reveals something about the worldview she inherited, her attitude toward her son, and probably her feelings about masturbation.[43]

Equally fascinating is the process by which the census board disciplined vernacular death into something scientific. Working with physicians, De Bow took the vast catalog of self-reported causes and winnowed them down to a list of 148, mostly by combining cases that were referred to by synonymous popular names. De Bow then sent this "translated and condensed catalogue" to Edward Jarvis, the Harvard-trained physician making a national reputation in nosology. Peeved that the list had already been massaged, Jarvis urged that in future years the Census Office create a national network of local physicians who could translate disease names common in their region into something more useful. Nevertheless he went to work, further winnowing De Bow's list from 148 to 114. Chicken pox, diseases of the eyes, herpes, hives, mumps, ringworm, tetter, and a host of other maladies, he said, were simply not fatal. Some of these cases could be recategorized; anyone who died of chicken pox, for instance, probably died of smallpox, and these cases could be filed under "diseases of the skin." In other instances, he said, the diagnoses were so epiphenomenal that whatever did the killing should be listed as "unknown." (Jarvis was on the fence about masturbation. "Onanism," he said, "possibly, but not probably, was a cause of death. It wastes life and produces other disorders [but] cases under this head should be put under the unknown." Despite this, a lone New Mexican masturbator ran the bureaucratic gauntlet to officially die of 'onanism.')[44]

Whatever the problems and occasional ridiculousness of the first mortality census, something important had been achieved. From screw threads to railroad gauges to currency, standardization was both product and producer of modernity, and in the first federal health survey, Kennedy, Shattuck, De Bow, and Jarvis had begun the process of disciplining death itself to bureaucratic categories. "There never has been, and there may not be again," Jarvis wrote De Bow, "another opportunity, such as you now enjoy, of showing to the world the . . . names of diseases which are found in the several States and thought to be fatal." For his part, De Bow finally came around to understanding that something miraculous had been achieved. Here was a scale of death never before documented so precisely; here was death aggregated and disciplined into neat little columns. Here were "one-third of a million people scattered over three millions of square miles of territory," all making their varied way to the grave in a single year. "The value of such a multitude of facts cannot but be very great, even although they do not constitute the whole of them," De Bow concluded. "We are every day accustomed to draw deductions for the whole from a part, and to argue out the true and complete from the approximate and uncertain."[45]

Nineteenth-century statisticians weren't accustomed to interpolating from approximate and uncertain data. We are—and the results are chilling. Take, for instance, the staggering number of Americans who apparently died of simple vitamin deficiencies in 1850. While they wouldn't and couldn't have known it, most of the deaths recorded as black tongue, chlorosis, jaundice, rickets, scurvy, and perhaps even dirt-eating could have been cured with a multivitamin or a better diet. Sadder still, the South Carolina data reveal that Black people were 53.5 times more likely to die of suffocation than white people, 47.2 times more likely to die of cholera, and almost five times more likely to die of worms or of burning. What can be made of such discrepancies? The "suffocation" deaths were probably cases in which planters and physicians believed careless enslaved mothers had rolled over their infants in their sleep, thereby suffocating them. Most of these cases were probably crib death, or SIDS, news that would have come as cold comfort to enslaved mothers who were told that they had, purposely or not, killed their own children. The "cholera" deaths are likewise baffling until we note the one disease that disproportionately affected white people—yellow fever. In the racist understanding of Black biology, Black people were "habituated, from infancy, to the combined impression of atmospheric heat and miasma" and thereby enjoyed a "general exemption from bilious and hepatic diseases" like yellow fever.[46] This scientific mumbo jumbo may explain why so many Black people were listed as having died from cholera—because they were not allowed to die from yellow fever. Like the self-reported assessments on which they were based, the "scientific" categorizations of the mortality census were simultaneously a deeply flawed index of nineteenth-century mortality and a deeply informative index of nineteenth-century racial assumptions. Black people were probably not twice as likely to die of old age, for example; white people were simply more likely to attribute Black death to a body that just gave out. In other categories, however, we can imagine that the mortality census actually did capture medical truths. Black people were probably more likely to be burned or to drown. Diagnosis in such cases is relatively straightforward. Exhausted and living in fire traps, they probably did disproportionately burn to death. And while the enslaved probably never died *of* worms, they did die more often *with* worms because they had no shoes and walked in dirt contaminated with feces and soil-transmitted helminths, hookworms, and whipworms.[47]

There are ways, moreover, to check the mortality census's supposed bad data against known history. Take, for example, the case of murder. According to the 1850 mortality census, the per capita murder capital of America was California, followed quickly by Texas, Florida, Arkansas, Georgia, Kentucky, Louisiana, Alabama, Tennessee, Virginia, Mississippi, North Carolina, South Carolina, and Missouri. With a seven-to-one ratio of males to females, in a state where gold had just been discovered and law enforcement was minimal, California probably *was* a murder palace. And the fact that every state thereafter was southern? This couldn't have been information that De Bow *wanted* to reveal, but it certainly rings true. Or take the case of suicide. The states with the highest per capita rates of self-destruction in 1850 were New Hampshire, Massachusetts, Maine, Vermont, Connecticut, Rhode Island, New York, and Iowa. Were cold, gray winters responsible, or were northerners more likely to *admit* that a suicide had taken place in their household? We don't know. But this is why data is collected in the first place. Because without it, you can't ask good questions.[48]

More important than all this: bad data is good data if one wants to tell the story told here—the conceptual history of how the data got better. Looking back from 1943 on a public health revolution he'd witnessed (and contributed to), Charles-Edward Winslow said, "There are many approaches to the study of medical history. [To me] the most fascinating . . . has been the history of ideas, the slow and gradual evolution of human thought." As Winslow would have appreciated, such a history is complete only if it also includes the history of how bad ideas were overcome—what Steven Johnson has called the "sociology of error," or what we might call "misepistemology"—the science of understanding why smart people, committed to logic and working at the top of their game, got so much wrong. The 1850 mortality census may have been an unmitigated disaster, but here's the thing: it was a start.[49]

During the Civil War, the 1860 mortality census was calculated and released by census boys who might have been sent to the killing fields but were instead dragooned to make maps and tabulate data for the War Department. "No military expedition was ever based on sounder or surer data," said Sherman as he embarked on his March to the Sea. Armed with maps displaying county-level grain yields and enslaved populations, Sherman turned data into actionable military intelligence: "I had the Census statistics showing the produce of every county through which I designed to pass," he told a friend.[50]

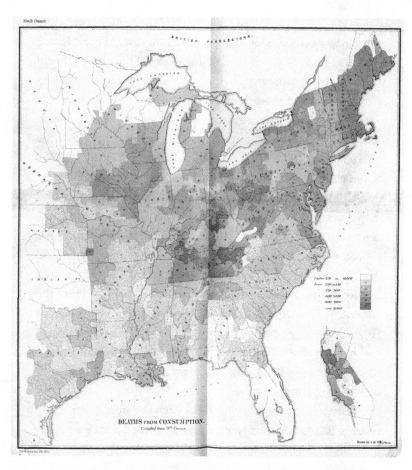

DEATHS FROM CONSUMPTION.
Compiled from 9th Census

By 1880, the federal mortality census featured choropleth
maps like this, displaying per capita deaths by consumption.
*The Vital Statistics of the United States, Ninth Census (June 1, 1870),*
vol. 2 (Washington, DC: Government Printing Office, 1872).

During the 1870 census, public health statistics (and the real
threats to humankind) again took a back seat to the bigger issue
in census politics: the question of how many former slaves there
actually were in the South. (This is an irony we don't often think
about, but the end of the Three-Fifths Compromise effectively
*increased* the representation of the ex-Confederate states in

Congress. If they could deny Black people the right to vote, white supremacists could achieve two-fifths more power.) For all these wretched politics, however, data has a way of pushing back and revealing the truth: what divides us politically can never be as strong as what unites us biologically; whatever enemies we find within ourselves, they are never so great a threat as the enemy that recognizes our common humanity even when we can't: the microbes that answer only to natural logic. And so in the 1880s, at the nadir of American race relations, census personnel produced some of the nation's first-ever attempts to visualize and map disease hot spots, because the data had revealed that place, not race, was a better indicator of human health outcomes. In 1888, the Census Office sponsored a contest to see who could design the fastest data-tabulating machine, and the winner was a former census employee, Herman Hollerith, the founder of the American Tabulating Machine Company, later consolidated as IBM. However grotesque its flaws and assumptions, the census had become the "Big Data" project of the nineteenth century, driving a data industry that got bigger, better, and faster, ultimately producing the supercomputer.[51]

Resistance to data collection has been endemic to American history. In 1986, Arthur Kellermann published a modest study in the *New England Journal of Medicine*, noting that every time someone committed a gun-related homicide in self-defense, the same sample of guns produced forty-three suicides, criminal homicides, or mortal accidents. Put another way, guns in the home were forty-three times more likely to produce a sad and unintended outcome than an outcome the NRA would celebrate. Kellermann sought only to treat guns as a public health issue, but his findings threatened a central tenet of the NRA's philosophy: the gun as a pure "good." In 1996, Republican congressman Jay Dickey successfully introduced a rider into an omnibus spending bill stating that "none of the funds made available for injury prevention and control at the Centers for Disease Control and Prevention (CDC) may be used to advocate or promote gun control." This had a chilling effect on research, and for twenty years, public health officials were effectively hamstrung from gathering data about gun-related homicides and suicides.[52]

In 2020, testing for COVID-19 in the United States fell radically behind that of any comparable country. "Testing is a double-edged sword," Trump told the crowd in Oklahoma. "Here's the bad part: When you do testing to that extent, you're gonna find more people, you're gonna find more cases [so] I said to my people, 'Slow the testing down, please.'" "Trump wants to keep people from getting tested so the official case load in the U.S. remains artificially low," reported Amanda Marcotte for *Salon*. "There's no need to tiptoe around the situation here. Trump . . . wants to artificially deflate a number he thinks makes him look bad."[53]

We've seen this before. In the 1850s, slaveholders declared slavery a "positive good," but when statisticians sought to gather the data that might prove them right or wrong, they kneecapped the statisticians and deep-sixed any effort to plumb the numbers. Today's resistance to datafication comes from the same place: the recognition that data exposes bad-faith arguments. This isn't how science is supposed to work. If, as a society, we can somehow justify enslaving people or bearing the burden of first-grade gun slaughters or dying in droves rather than wearing a mask, that may technically be our right. But we do not get to not count the dead.

In 2012, Prabhat Jha—Endowed Chair in Disease Control at University of Toronto and a senior scientist for the World Health Organization—argued that more than a century and a half after Lemuel Shattuck's seminal report, "counting the dead [remains] one of the world's best investments to reduce premature mortality." "About 56 million deaths occur worldwide every year," Jha noted. And yet while "certification of deaths with causes assigned by physicians is nearly universal for the 8 million deaths occurring in developed countries, [death registration] is low among the 48 million deaths in developing countries." Jha's solution for developing nations today is the same as Shattuck's solution for 1850s Massachusetts: count the dead.[54]

# TWO

# ᶠHE MATH OF AFTER

*Only the dead have seen the end of war.*

GEORGE SANTAYANA

N February 1, 1864, the Confederate blockade runner *Presto* collided with a partially submerged wreck in Charleston Harbor. *Presto*'s captain had run off, and Confederate colonel Lawrence Keitt was charged with recovering the ship's cargo under heavy fire from federal gunboats. When a shell landed twenty feet from Keitt, he gave himself up for dead before realizing the fuse had not detonated.[1]

For the next several days, amid explosive founts of salt water and sand, Keitt and his men managed to recover the bulk of the shoes, blankets, flannels, pork, and beef the *Presto* had been carrying. Keitt wanted to distribute the supplies to his exhausted and bedraggled soldiers, but his superiors forced him to return it all to a central depot. The incident was the last straw in a war Keitt was beginning both to hate and to accept responsibility for. As a congressman, Keitt had been the fiercest of the fire-eaters,

## VERY LATEST.

### Another Terrible Battle on Tuesday.

### Advices Up to Wednesday Morning at 10 O'clock.

WASHINGTON, Wednesday, May 11.

A distinguished officer arrived here about 10 o'clock to-night who was present during the terrible conflict of yesterday afternoon and last evening, and who left Gen. GRANT in the saddle as late as ten o'clock this morning. He sums up the bloody work of yesterday thus:

The fight opened all along the lines. LONGSTREET's corps, under HILL, held the rebel right resting about two miles northeast of Spottsylvania, and GRANT attacked BURNSIDE's Ninth Corps against it. At a given moment, later in the afternoon, BURNSIDE precipitated his entire command against the second and third troops, upon the rebel right-defying and completely resisting it, capturing three rebel brigades and four pieces of cannon. The fight continued with a fiercely never before witnessed until 9 o'clock last night, when it closed upon the bloodiest field produced in this war. The losses on both sides are stated to be very large. Of the three rebel brigades captured, some escaped during the awful carnage which followed, but twelve hundred of the captures were sent to the rear this morning. Our informant talked with some of them before leaving to-day, and they acknowledged that they had been in every principal battle of the war, but had never experienced such terrible fighting. The battle ceased at about 9 o'clock, our lines having advanced, BURNSIDE occupying, at the end of the conflict, the intrenchments held by LONGSTREET's forces in the beginning. This morning the fight was not renewed up to 10 o'clock, at which time BURNSIDE held the same position. Lee's army was then contracted into a sort of horse shoe form in and about the town known as Spottsylvania Court-house. Gen. STEVENSON, of Massachusetts, is killed. The reports that Gens. BURNSIDE and WADSWORTH have both been killed have been unfounded and the other killed are many. BURNSIDE's movements north of Richmond have been felt and appreciated.

### ANOTHER DISPATCH.

WASHINGTON, Wednesday, May 11.

I have just received intelligence that LEE has been compelled to withdraw from Spottsylvania Court-house. He was danced on both right and left. The fighting was terrible yesterday. The rebels retreated across the South Anna River. GRANT is in pursuit.

### THE CASUALTIES.

WASHINGTON, Wednesday, May 11.

The following additional casualties are reported:—all wounded except those categorized KILLED.

*By 1864, newspapers had achieved "onomastic density," featuring something entirely new: long lists of common people who were hurting or dead. "The Casualties," New York Times, May 12, 1864. Courtesy of The New York Times.*

thundering about the positive good of slavery and pounding on his congressional desk until "John Adams's extracts shuddered under the blows." As the war ground on, however, Keitt at last acknowledged his own hubris. "I had as much to do probably as anyone else in bringing [this] about," he noted glumly, "and I must accept its consequences. I see thousands around me who knew nothing about it, who had but little at stake, and who hoped to gain but little. They were carried by us into the war and they are fighting it out. I can do no less." Keitt was blown off his horse at Cold Harbor. His last words were "oh wife, wife."[2]

The Civil War leveled everyone. The war leveled Atlanta and Columbia, burnt down Barnum's American Museum, created a national cemetery of Robert E. Lee's estate, and liberated a third of the South. The war laid waste to millions of acres of farmland and forest, destroyed two-thirds of Southern wealth, slaughtered two-fifths of the region's livestock, killed one-third of the white Southerners who fought in it (one-quarter of the Confederacy's white males of military age), and freed four million people (13 percent of the country's entire population). The war swept three million men into military service, giving most of them a pension while killing the rest—750,000 men, roughly as many as in all of America's other wars combined. And the men who made it through the war had the scars to prove it. Some wounds were physical, inadequately dressed and treated. A hundred thousand men literally left a piece of themselves on the battlefield, and countless others would never piss right, crap right, or have sex again. Other wounds were psychological. Having fired one of the first shots of the war, famed fire-eater Edmund Ruffin fired one of the last shots of the war—putting a bullet in his brain pan— blazing a trail for the thousand veterans who followed suit. Many nights James Chesnut, husband of the famed diarist Mary Chesnut, slouched off to the porch to drink himself into a gray haze because the porch was where his wife wanted him to be. "I am not worthy to live," soldier Edwin Fay wrote his wife in 1862.

"I am unfit to die. My heart has become harder than the nether Mill Stone. . . . If I come home, I think I shall bivouac for the future in your flower yard." Perhaps that was as close as Fay dared dream of being to something so much softer than himself.[3]

Accounting for the Civil War's damage is a fool's errand, but we are obligated to try. For a comparable impact on today's population, eight million people would have to die—roughly the population of New York City or the entire state of Georgia. We would have to endure a 9/11 every day for four years. We would be accountable to more than a million American amputees; thirty million veterans would be coming home; thirty-five million ex-slaves would be looking for work, spouses, children, educations, hope; thirty-three million Americans would be mourning an immediate family member. "The war," wrote Ralph Waldo Emerson, "has assumed such huge proportions that it threatens to engulf us all—no preoccupation can exclude it & no hermitage hide us."[4]

The war was leveling in every sense that matters. Jefferson had famously trembled for his country when he reflected that God was just and his justice wouldn't sleep forever. In his second inaugural address, Abraham Lincoln struck the right tone: Having endured slavery for so long, God's justice had awoken, and he intended to mete it out Old Testament style—fortune was to be repaid by misfortune, and all debts were to be sunk in blood. The nation's attitude, Lincoln said, should be that of any other sinner whom God seeketh to chasten—it should submit, and then move more humbly forward, "with malice toward none, with charity for all."[5]

For an incredibly short time, Americans were truly chastened by their Civil War. Whatever else the war produced—bloated bond markets, price gouging, and rampant prostitution—it created, for the merest of moments, a humbler people. "I have been driven many times upon my knees," Lincoln supposedly said, "by the overwhelming conviction that I had nowhere else to go."[6]

Catastrophes have always invited politicians, opportunists, and survivors sick with grief to secure someone else to blame. The best of us have another impulse: count the dead.

Clara Barton is widely lionized as the founder of the American Red Cross and an "American Nightingale" for her volunteer work as a medical organizer during the Civil War. In 1975, the National Park Service established the Clara Barton National Historic Site in Glen Echo, Maryland—the first NPS museum dedicated to the accomplishments of a woman and a site that remains a monument to her humanitarian achievements. Only in 1997, however, did a carpenter rediscover Barton's other brainchild, the Missing Soldiers Office, which was designed to number and name the Civil War dead. After having stood boarded up in Washington, D.C., for decades, the office opened as a second Barton museum in 2015, with hordes of Barton's records still stored in the attic. Such neglect is unsurprising. "Barton the caretaker" seemed easier to commemorate than "Barton the bureaucrat." I would argue, however, that in a long life otherwise dedicated to humanitarian aid, Barton's short stint at the Missing Soldiers Office is the key to unlocking her character. Like most who are exceptionally successful at saving lives, Barton became debilitatingly fixated on the lives she did not save. Whereas Union general George G. Meade could leave the "debris" behind at Gettysburg—a euphemism for his unburied dead—Barton marinated in the aftermath. Better than any general, she saw the war at two scales simultaneously. Sitting at the head of a thousand beds, she watched as one man or another died or didn't, and they all became individuals—because they had mothers, fathers, siblings, and dreams. And gradually, inevitably, they all became interchangeable—because we all have mothers, fathers, siblings, and dreams. This twin sensitivity to scale—granularity and enormity held simultaneously in the human mind—became her outstanding quality. Standing at Andersonville prison after

Hovering over Andersonville is Death itself, skeletal prisoners burying more skeletal corpses. Thomas O'Dea, *Andersonville Prison, Camp Sumter, Ga.*, ca. 1885, lithograph, 39.88×60.25 in. Courtesy of Library of Congress.

its evacuation, Barton had only to study the pockmarked ground where thousands of men had made their homes and ends in the mud to feel the entire weight of the travesty. "I have looked upon [war's] terrible face," she later said, "but friends, not in the same breath in which I would speak of anything else in the Heavens above, or the earth beneath, would I speak of this. . . . My heart sickened and stood still, my brain whirled, and the light of my eyes went out, and I said surely this was not the gate of hell, but hell itself."[7]

This telescopic sense of scale, an ability to extrapolate from one person in pain to a thousand without psychic numbing, turns out to be rare. Rarer still was Barton's instinctive response: Make a list. Count the dead. Record the names. In her efforts at the Missing Soldiers Office, Barton was helped enormously by a young man with a similar impulse: former Union private Dorence Atwater. Atwater had been captured at Gettysburg and sent to Andersonville, where his fine penmanship was rewarded with the job of processing and recording the name of every prisoner who died. At war's end, Atwater smuggled his list out of "hell itself" and became so obsessed with publishing it that he willingly suffered a court-martial (and a return to jail) rather than surrender it to a commander he was sure would let the list molder.

Thanks in part to Barton, Atwater was eventually released, and in the spring of 1866, the *New York Tribune* published his entire list, all thirteen thousand names. "This Record was originally copied for you," Atwater told the public, "because I feared that neither you nor the Government of the United States would ever otherwise learn the fate of your *loved ones* whom I saw daily dying before me. I could do nothing for them, but I resolved that I would at least try to let you sometime know when and how they died."[8]

Ultimately, the Missing Soldiers Office had to strike the tent. The job was too big, and Barton and Atwater were given too

# A LIST

OF THE

# UNION SOLDIERS BURIED AT ANDERSONVILLE.

All Persons numbered below 12367, died in 1864; above that number, in 1865. All names with a *, denote Corporal; those with a †, Sergeant.

## ALABAMA.

No. of Grave.

7584, Barton, Wm, 1 cav, Co L, died Sept 1, scorbutus.
2111, Berry, J M, † 1 cav, Co A, died May 17, diarrhœa c.
4372, Balls, Robt, 1 cav, Co A, died Aug 5, dysentery.
5505, Boobur, Wm, 1 cav, Co E, died Aug 15, diarrhœa.
8425, Brice, J C, 1 cav, Co L, died Sept 11, scorbutus.

8147, Guthrie, J, 1 cav, Co I, died Sept 8, scorbutus.

2514, Henry, P, 1 cav, Co F, died June 26, pneumonia.

930, Jones, Jno F, 1 cav, Co K, died Mar 15, anasarca.

4215, Mitchel, Jno D, 1, Co A, died Aug 4, scorbutus.

5077, Ponders, J, 1 cav, Co H, died Aug 8, diarrhœa.
5763, Panier, R, 1 Co L, died Aug 15, diarrhœa.
6886, Patterson, W D, 1, Co K, died Aug 25, diarrhœa s.
2504, Prett, J R, 1, Co F, died June 26, diarrhœa s.

10000, Redman, W R, 1 cav, Co G, died Oct 14, scorbutus.

4731, Stubbs, W, 1, Co I, died Aug 4, bronchitis.

## CONNECTICUT.

2290, Anderson, A, 14, Co B, died June 23, diarrhœa c.

3467, Batchelder, Benj, 16, Co C, died July 17, diarrhœa a.
5964, Bary, John, 16, Co C, died July 19, diarrhœa c.
7896, Brackinsett, H, 14, Co D, died Aug 20, dysentery.
2833, Brennion, M, 14, Co B, died July 3, dysentery c.
3721, Burns, Jno, 7, Co L, died July 12, diarrhœa.
10414, Bloualy, E, 8, Co D, died Oct 6, scorbutus.
945, Bigelow, Wm, 7, Co B, died April 14, diarrhœa.
11965, Bill, H A, 3, Co B, died Nov 11, scorbutus.
12080, Brookmeyer, T W, 8, Co H, died Nov 18, scorbutus.
12152, Burke B, 16, Co D, died Nov 24, scorbutus.
1299, Bone, A, 1 Co E, died Dec 1, scorbutus.
1062, Barnham F, † 14, Co I, died Oct 11, dysentery c.
4692, Barlow, O L, 16, Co E, died Oct 13, dysentery a.
10878, Bennett, N, 1s, Co H, died Oct 12, scorbutus.
4826, Brown, C H, 1, Co H, died Aug 15, dysentery.
4912, Boyce, Wm, 7, Co B, died Aug 17, dysentery.
6883, Bishop, B H, 1 cav, Co D, died Aug 18, dysentery.
6181, Bushnell, Wm, 14, Co D, died Aug 10, cerebritis.
7105, Bailey, F, 16, Co E, died Sept 4, dysentery.
2954, Brewer, O E, 21, Co A, died June 16, diarrhœa c.
5590, Burns, D, 6, Co G, died Aug 14, bronchitis.
5432, Bolough, 11, Co B, died Aug 14, diarrhœa.
5754, Boots, Jas, 4, 16, Co A, died Aug 15, dysentery.
11556, Bidwell, D, 16, Co D, died Oct 28, scorbutus.
4256, Bakeslee, H, 1 cav, Co L, died July 20, anasarca.
3808, Bishop, A, 18, Co A, died July 24, dysentery.
3493, Bossmore, Peter, 14, Co B, died Jan 2, diarrhœa.
2759, Babcock, H, 20, Co A, died July 1, scorbutus.
2878, Baldwin, Thomas, 1 cav, Co L, died July 3, 9 cumonia.
2286, Boswyoth, A M, 16, Co F, died July 3, diarrhœa c.
5152, Bangor, John, 11, Co C, died Aug 5, dysentery.
5193, Brooks, Wm D, † 16, Co F, died Aug 9, dysentery.
5538, Bower, John, 10, Co F, died Aug 11, scorbutus.
5452, Bently, F, 6, Co H, died Aug 12, diarrhœa.

5464, Bently, James, 1 cav, Co I, died Aug 12, scorbutus.
4890, Blackman, A, † 2 artil, Co C, died Aug 6, scorbutus.
7742, Brosley, B F, 16, Co E, died Sept 3, dysentery.
8078, Ballentine, Robert, 16, Co A, died Sept 6, dysentery.
12408, Bassett, J B, 11, Co B, died Jan 6, 65, scorbutus.
12540, Bohine, C, 3, Co E, died Jan 27, '65, rheumatism.
1829, Bennie Charles, 7, Co K, died Feb 8, scorbutus.

3757, Chapin, J L, 16, Co A, died July 21, '64, fever intermittent.
3809, Cottrell, F, 7, Co C, died July 25, diarrhœa c.
4901, Carleton, ---, 11, Co B, died July 25, scorbutus.
4967, Cutler, M, 7, Co E, died July 25, diarrhœa.
4449, Connor, D, 18, Co F, died Aug 1, scorbutus.
4848, Carrer, D B, 16, Co D, died Aug 8, diarrhœa c.
5660, Cook, W H, 1 cav, Co G, died Aug 18, cerebritis.
6152, Clark, H H, 16, Co B, died Aug 10, cerebritis.
6846, Clark, W, 6, Co A, died Aug 25, diarrhœa.
5799, Champlain, H, 10, Co F, died Aug 15, dysentery.
336, Cane, John, 9, Co H, died April 2, diarrhœa.
629, Christian, A M, 1, Co A, died April 19, dysentery.
778, Crawford, James, 14, Co A, died April 26, diarrhœa c.
1316, Chapman M, 16, Co E, died Aug 30, scorbutus.
7548, Cleary, P, 1 cav, Co B, died Aug 31, scorbutus.
7790, Campbell, Robt, 7, Co E, died Aug 31, diarrhœa.
7418, Calter, M, 16, Co K, died Aug 31, diarrhœa.
7685, Carver, John G, 16, Co B, died Sept 2, dysentery.
7789, Cam, Thomas, 14, Co G, died Sept 4, diarrhœa.
9684, Conney, B, 8, Co G, died Sept 29, scorbutus.
4072, Cutter, W, 18, Co B, died Oct 3, diarrhœa.
11175, Callahand, 11, Co I, died Oct 18, scorbutus.
11361, Candee, D, M, 2 artil, Co A, died Oct 23, scorbutus.

25, Dowd, F, 7, Co I, died March 8, pneumonia.
1825, Day s, Wm D cav, Co L, died Aug 50, dysentery.
2413, Davis, W, 10, Co E, died July 3, anasarca.
3614, Damery, John, 6, Co A, died July 29, diarrhœa.

little help. Atwater became consul to Tahiti, married a Tahitian princess, and made a fortune. Barton went on to immortality as the founder of the American Red Cross. Too frail herself to be present at Atwater's funeral in 1910, she sent along a tribute to his service. "And what was that service?" she asked rhetorically. "The glories of combat? The pride and pomp of armies? . . . Nay, nay, good friends. None of that. In place of these he brought you a few crumpled sheets of paper, whereon with an arm skeletonized by hunger and the lack of every comfort and need of human life, but the breath that sustained it, he had traced and preserved the names and last earthly records of 13,000 dead comrades, left in strange and unknown graves."[9]

Bearing helpless witness to a demographic disaster, Barton and Atwater had responded instinctively, which is to say clerically. In the process, they had hit upon one of the simplest and most effective ways to render simultaneously the twin scales of human catastrophe: the list.

The historian Drew Gilpin Faust has written deeply and movingly about how Civil War soldiers and their kin improvised many of the functions we now associate with the federal government when its army is at war. Grieving mothers, fathers, and wives competed with looters amid the carnage of every battle's aftermath, searching for their boys. "Now I am content," wrote Jane Deans after traveling with a babe in arms to retrieve her husband's corpse, "for his 5 littel orphans can go with me to see where their Fathers bones do ly." After Gettysburg, a reporter described a sobbing widow digging up grave after grave until "her heart almost failed." During the Civil War, notifying next of kin was the job of whichever grieving friend was brave enough to write the family. Without dog tags, soldiers wrote their names on slips of paper and pinned them to their backs, so they would be easier to identify.[10]

Of all the war's improvisations, however, it was the casualty list that became the most macabre and meaningful way

Americans processed the consequences of modern war. Both Union and Confederate armies required officers to keep track of the killed, wounded, and missing from their units, but the records were poorly maintained, and no one considered sharing them with the public. This left to the newspapers the job of satisfying public demand for reliable information about who had been killed. The result was newspapers flooded with what one scholar has called "onomastic density"—long lists of names. The novel experience of scanning the lists made a profound impression on the culture. One of the more popular poems of the time was the anonymously authored "Reading the List," in which a woman asks a man standing behind a fanned-open newspaper a simple question:

> "Is there any news of the war?" she said.
> "Only a list of the wounded and dead,"
>> Was the man's reply
>> Without lifting his eye
> To the face of the woman standing by;
> "'Tis the very thing I want," she said:
> "Read me the list of the wounded and dead."
>
>> *Unknown*

In a similar tableau, Herman Melville captured a large group of excited men, gathered around the newspaper office to hear the latest from the battlefield, shouting at the news of victory. Only when they depart do we understand that women were in the crowd also, hanging around to devour the cast-off pages that hadn't been read:

> But others were who wakeful laid
> In midnight beds, and early rose,
> And feverish in the foggy snows,
> Snatched the damp paper—wife and maid.
> The death-list like a river flows

Down the pale sheet,
And there the whelming waters meet.

*Herman Melville*

"We see the list in the morning paper at breakfast," noted one reviewer of Mathew Brady's photographic exhibit *The Dead of Antietam*, "but dismiss its recollection with the coffee. There is a confused mass of names, but they are all strangers; we forget the horrible significance that dwells amid the jumble of type."[11]

 The casualty list as we know it was invented in ancient Athens. Having erected the world's first democracy, Athenians immediately faced the problem of how they would remember their dead *equally*. Mnemonics itself—the art of memory—was created as a result of a catastrophe: the collapse of a building. Hired by a local potentate to entertain dinner guests, the poet Simonides was just getting through a throat-clearing toast to the gods when his host stopped him. Why not move on to the toast of the host? Simonides hesitated before being called away by messengers at the door. Standing on the porch, the entire building collapsed behind him, mangling the host and guests beyond recognition. The story is a classic Greek tale, alive with hubris and tragic flaws and divine whim. But something Athenian happened in the aftermath. As the ruin swarmed with confused mourners, Simonides closed his eyes and, brick by brick, resurrected the whole marble edifice in his imagination: who *precisely* had been sitting where? When he opened his eyes, he led each mourner to their particular dead.[12]

Thus was born the memory palace—the conceptual mode by which massive amounts of information are committed to memory by proceeding *spatially* through a figurative structure. Today, mental athletes use this same technique to remember a random sequence of cards or digits of pi to the hundred-thousandth place. What gets forgotten in the process is the original function of the method itself: a means of remembering the dead. Simonides had to remember only a few dozen casualties. As Athenians became embroiled in the Persian Wars, they faced the prospect of remembering not a few dozen friends but a few thousand strangers, and their memorial task multiplied out of hand. This is why they created the casualty list, a list meant to inform and *be performed*. As classicist Andrej Petrovic has explained, in Athenian culture catalogs (*kataloge*) of the killed had existed before: the names of the nine soldiers cut down by Hector or the seven soldiers killed by Odysseus or Achilles. Not until the Greco-Persian Wars did the Athenians create the casualty list as we know it—a list of names and names only, thrown upon the public conscience with minimal commentary. Studying the way the names were abbreviated and arranged epigraphically, Petrovic has concluded that the lists were designed not only to be etched into stone but also to be memorized and performed as poetry. It has long been known that Herodotus committed to memory the names of all three hundred Spartans killed at Thermopylae. The original questions among classicists were where he learned the names, when, and from whom. For Andrej Petrovic, the more important questions were why and how. As a democracy, the Athenians had concluded that their obligation to the fallen was both clerical and memorial: they had to remember *everyone* who had fallen *by name*. Simonides's principle of *loci memoriae*, then, was not a mnemonic exercise or a parlor trick; rather, it was an act of democratic conscience. When Athenian general Cimon returned home from his victory against the Persians, he asked the assembly for his reward. They offered him the highest honor they knew to bestow—three marked stones in the Stoa of the Herms bearing only the names of his fallen men. A visitor to the shrine famously asked, "Is the name of the general anywhere here?" "Nowhere," came the reply, "only the names of the people."[13]

In grappling with their dead, Barton and Atwater had not invented a new form; rather, they had reinvented the one we continuously manage to forget as we seek to enshrine the "horrible significance that dwells amid the jumble of type." And for a while it works. "A glance at the published pamphlet," Herman Melville said of Barton and Atwater's Andersonville volume, "conveys a feeling mournfully impressive. Seventy-four large double-columned pages in fine print. Looking through them is like getting lost among the old turbaned head-stones and cypresses in the interminable Black Forest of Scutari [the famous tree graveyard in Constantinople]."[14]

All great wars have a memorial half-life. Inevitably, moral clarity decays. In *Civil War Monuments and the Militarization of America*, Thomas J. Brown exhaustively catalogs changes over time in the sentiment and style of monuments erected after the conflict, moving inevitably from accountability to elision. In the immediate postwar period, most towns put up modest markers with a simple objective: memorializing their human losses. "The listing of fallen soldiers' names," Brown notes, "was so essential that some communities considered nothing else necessary." The decorative elements that accompanied the lists, if any, were somber, chiseled without ornamentation or patriotic frippery. If the marker depicted a soldier, his eyes were as downcast as his gun, his bayonet in the ground, his chin on the butt, as if to say he was tired of war. Once these markers were erected, monument building slipped into decline. "The number of monuments unveiled in New England between 1870 and 1874," Brown notes, "fell by a third from the total installed during 1863–69 and then again by a half between 1875 and 1879."[15]

And then a strange thing happened. Beginning in 1880, monument building in the North and South accelerated and then went into overdrive. "The number of common-soldier monuments unveiled across the country during the first fifteen years of the twentieth century," Brown notes, "was almost double that of the pervious fifteen years." No longer were soldiers depicted with downcast eyes. They bore flags aloft, guns at the ready. No longer did monuments feature a list of the dead; the new focus was war's glory, not its cost. Equestrian statues proliferated, generals sitting imperiously astride their war horses. Like Rome, the United States had become an empire, seeking to project its military power.[16]

The national chastening had been difficult to sustain. Americans had been eager to return to their lives, their verities, their profits. Over the course of a decade, they moved quickly from atonement to commemoration to celebration as they transformed their Civil War from *Odyssey*—a returning home to devastation, betrayal, revenge, and forgiveness—to *Iliad*—a national morality play rooted in epic mythmaking. In the process, Civil War monuments moved from commemorative lists of the dead to shrines of self-appreciation erected for the living.

 In August 1865, New York author John Townsend Trowbridge was seized by a sudden desire to tour the war-torn states of the South. He wanted to see for himself "the most noted battle-fields of the war." He wanted to interview "officers and soldiers of both sides." He wanted to follow "in the track of the destroying armies." Most important, he wanted to make "a record of actual observations and conversations, free from fictitious coloring . . . endeavoring, at all times and in all places, to receive correct impressions of the country, of its inhabitants, [and] of the great contest of arms just closed." He was, in a sense, the war's first tourist, and its first historian. And his first stop, as it continues to be for many Americans seeking a first taste of the Civil War, was Gettysburg.[17]

"Gettysburg is . . . pleasantly situated on the swells of a fine undulating country," Trowbridge noted upon his arrival in the village. But about the town itself, he said, "There is nothing very interesting. It consists chiefly of two-story houses of wood and brick, in dull rows, with thresholds but little elevated above the street." Gettysburg's existence, he decided, owed "to the mere fact that several important roads found it convenient to meet at this point, to which accident also is due its historical renown. The circumstance which made it a burg made it likewise a battle-field."[18]

After touring that battlefield, Trowbridge took a stroll through the cemetery, which was actually becoming quite lovely. Two years before, a visitor would have seen "festering corpses at every step; some still unburied; some [so] hastily and rudely buried [that] the appearance presented was almost as repulsive as where no attempt at burial had been made." But by August 1865, the shallow trenches and wooden marker boards had been replaced by ordered graves and gravestones. The gate and gatehouse were complete, iron fences and low stone walls marked the cemetery boundaries, and a macadamized road lolled through the main avenue. There were as yet, however, no headstones for the "unknowns." "Their resting-places were indicated by a forest of stakes," Trowbridge noted. He continued,

> I have seen few sadder sights. . . . Each man had his history; each soldier resting here had his interests, his loves, his darling hopes, the same as you or I. All were laid down with his life. It was no trifle to him, it was as great a thing to him as it would be to you, thus to be cut off from all things dear in this world, and to drop at once into a vague eternity. Grown accustomed to the waste of life through years of war, we learn to think too lightly of such sacrifices. "So many killed,"—with that brief sentence we glide over . . . unimaginably fearful fact[s]. [We] pass on to other details. We indulge in pious commonplaces.[19]

Trowbridge was right. Gettysburg had been the scene of "unimaginably fearful facts." And yet even as he wrote, those facts were being churned under by the "swells of a fine undulating country." Even as he wrote, the Battle of Gettysburg was cohering as a narrative more ordered than its cemetery. Edward Everett had added the storied ingredients at the cemetery's dedication: the tactical retreat through the village; the arrangement of the fish-hook-shaped defensive line; the fight for Little Round Top; the surge that broke at the Angle, saving Washington and the war. But it was Lincoln himself who did the most to purge the field of "grosser matter" in his Gettysburg Address. Speaking in aspirational abstractions about "honored dead," "hallowed ground," and a "new birth of freedom," Lincoln turned a bloodbath into a benediction.[20]

But what if he had made a list? What if he had named names? What if his list had started with Isaac Taylor, "hit in the top of the head by shell fragments which took off the back of his head and traveled down his body nearly cutting him in half." His brother Patrick cried as he buried him: "Well, Isaac, all I can give you is a soldier's grave." Alfred Sofield was bisected the other way; a shell "exploded under [his] prostrate form . . . and literally cut him in two, leaving his heels in contact with his head." Jefferson Copeland heard only a "stunning explosion" that left his entire shirt-front soaked in crimson. Sure he was dead, he gradually realized that it was the man beside him, Travis Maxey, who had supplied the blood: "The shell must have exploded inside of his body, as his neck, head, and the upper part of his chest were all gone, and he could be recognized only by his clothes."[21]

At Gettysburg, men had been shot through everything they had: nose, ear, throat, temple. Samuel Zook was so shredded by a shell that it "expos[ed] his heartbeats to observation." James McCleary was "so badly blown to pieces that . . . his ribs [were] broken open [and] you could see right into him." John Cranston was "shot in the gluteus," and in deference to his pain and ebbing life, his comrades pretended not to notice the foul stench emerging from the wound. And, of course, at Gettysburg as in Iraq and Afghanistan, men were hit "in the region of the loins"—the kind of obfuscating language preferred in after-action reports. Bob Crawford, also hit "in the region of the loins," was described as having received a mortal bowel wound passing through both hips. After the bullet went through him, Crawford took a mental inventory of his trousers and told his friends the truth: "Boys, I am ruined."[22]

All these men died at Gettysburg, and their ends were not pretty. Only generals get last words like, "Strike the tent" or "Let us cross over the river and rest under the shade of the trees." Lieutenant colonels get last words like, "Are you sure that is the order? Well, it is murder, but [I guess] it is the order." And privates get last words like, "Oh! God, I am shot" or "I am killed" or the more plaintive "Who shall care for Mother now?"[23]

Other last words at Gettysburg were sadder still. At Plum Run Valley, just west of Little Round Top, a shell took off the arm of Samuel Spear, a private in the Forty-Second Pennsylvania. Like a squirrel half run over in a road, Spear sprang up and ran around in circles as the blood spurted from his stump. "I won't die, I won't die," he cried before keeling over and dying. His leg broken by a bullet, Sumner Paine, the great-grandson of revolutionary legend Thomas Paine, fell to his knees in exasperation. "Isn't this glorious!" he screamed before a shell blew him apart. The last words of Jonathan Leavitt were more typical. His feet and ankles crushed by a cannon ball, Leavitt lay on the field unattended for forty hours, watching as his extremities turned into a black "mass of corruption." When finally carried to the amputation table, a doctor "passed his knife through the mass of flesh and bones and left his feet and ankles on the stretcher." Leavitt was "evidently aware of his critical condition, but anxious to live." His last words were simply, "Shall I pull through, Doctor?"[24]

And then there had been the men who tried to form last words but found, with mounting panic and confusion, that they could make only unintelligible noises. Shot through the heart, Charles Frederick Taylor had enough life and air left to raspingly ask his brother for water. But with the first swallow "blood began to come from his mouth & he seemed to want to say something. All [his brother] could understand was 'Mum' 'mum.'" "Nobody knows how dear Fred was to me," Bayard Taylor wrote of his "Mum-mumming" brother. "Through him I knew what a brother's love meant. I had brighter hopes for him than myself: he was better and nobler than I."[25]

This was the war Barton and Atwater had sought to capture in a list. In naked type, a list can seem clerical and reductive, but a list is one of the only data forms that is both microscopic and telescopic at the same. In a list, each name is the same—same font, same size, same type—and yet each name is different, representing a peculiar circumstance and tragedy. Each name is meaningful to a particular set of survivors, and yet the list has a repetitive and accumulating effect on anyone who bothers to read it. Everyone who scans it has to think: This one name among many could be the name of my son, my husband, my brother, or my sister, my daughter, my wife.

 At 9:45 A.M. on June 9, 1893, Charles E. Troutman was settling into his clerical desk at one of the subdivisions of the War Department; he had just dipped his pen into the red ink when he heard a "loud roar and a splitting crash." "I glanced upward," Troutman later told investigators, "and the [ceiling] was splitting across." With bricks and beams raining down, Troutman pushed his chair back only to realize that the floor was now collapsing beneath him as well. "It was absolute darkness when I got [out] from under this debris," Troutman told investigators, "and the dust was settling like lava. . . . I could not see my hand before me, and I scrambled and burroughed and [somehow] got out."[26]

Twenty-two clerks were not so lucky. Historians debate the cause of the collapse; probably it was the updates being done to the basement to install a generator for better lighting. The building in question, however, was the rehabbed Ford's Theatre. After Lincoln's assassination, no one had wanted to sit through another play at a crime scene, so Ford had sold out to the government. By 1893, the ramshackle building housed the Record and Pension Division of the War Department, which included the effort to number and name every Union soldier who died in the Civil War—an accumulating mass of paperwork. Metaphorically, the weight of the dead had multiplied out of hand; the effort to count them had collapsed.

And so, by degrees, the memory of a war's cost became shrouded in dust. Its gore was recast as a sacrifice to the higher purpose of condensing a nation, redeeming our sins, and rededicating us to freedom. Lincoln called the war "this fiery trial through which we pass." Shelby Foote called it the "cross-roads of our being." We never arrived at the more obvious conclusion: the war wasn't a test this country passed but a test we failed when we couldn't, short of war, give up our addiction to slavery.[27]

Violence is not the crucible in which national impurities are burned away. War does not clarify national purposes, and death does not reveal transcendent national truths. We realize this after every war, and then, with the passage of time, we forget it. In the wake of World War I, Western powers signed the Kellogg-Briand Pact, calling for the renunciation of war as an instrument of national policy. World War II followed, killing eighty-five million people, 3 percent of the globe. In the aftermath, the United Nations was created, devoted to saving mankind "from the scourge of war, which twice in our lifetime has brought untold sorrow to mankind."[28]

And yet more wars followed. In 1981, a twenty-one-year-old undergraduate, Maya Lin, beat out 1,441 other competitors with an unorthodox vision for a memorial: a black cut in the earth bearing the name of every American who had died in the Vietnam War. Her vision was controversial. Future senator Jim Webb, himself a veteran, said, "I never in my wildest dreams imagined such a nihilistic slab of stone." Others derided her design variously as a "black gash of sorrow and shame," "Orwellian glop," and a "wailing wall for future antidraft and antinuclear demonstrations." Tom Wolfe called the monument a "tribute to [activist] Jane Fonda" and a symbol of "a Red Guard–style Cultural Revolution," threatening to take over America. Ross Perot, a major donor to the Vietnam Veterans Memorial Fund, told the fund's president, "You've made a big, big mistake," and waged a three-year war to stop construction. (He also called Lin an "egg roll," just one of many attacks on her ethnicity and gender.)[29]

Lin couldn't talk about the controversy for almost two decades. "I needed to move past it," she said simply. But in 2000, she gave her first public account of the thought process behind her design:

> I think the most important aspect of the design . . . was that I had originally designed it for a class I was taking at Yale and not for the competition. In that sense, I had designed it for me—or, more exactly, for what I believed it should be. . . . The design emerged from an architectural seminar I was taking during my senior year. . . . The class, which was on funereal architecture, had spent the semester studying how people, through the built form, express their attitudes toward death. As a class, we thought the memorial was an appropriate design idea for our program, so we adopted it as our final design project. . . .
>
> As I did more research on monuments, I realized most carried larger, more general messages about a leader's victory or accomplishments rather than the lives lost. In fact, at the national level, individual lives were very seldom dealt with. . . .
>
> I made a conscious decision not to do any specific research on the Vietnam War and the political turmoil

surrounding it. I felt that the politics had eclipsed the veterans, their service, and their lives. I wanted to create a memorial that everyone would be able to respond to, regardless of whether one thought our country should or should not have participated in the war. The power of a name was very much with me at the time, partly because of the Memorial Rotunda at Yale. In Woolsey Hall, the walls are inscribed with the names of all the Yale alumni who have been killed in wars. I had never been able to resist touching the names cut into these marble walls, and no matter how busy or crowded the place is, a sense of quiet, a reverence, always surrounds those names. Throughout my freshman and sophomore years, the stonecutters were carving in by hand the names of those killed in the Vietnam War, and I think it left a lasting impression on me . . . the sense of the power of a name.[30]

Like Simonides, Barton, and Atwater before her, Lin had intuitively hit on the power of a complete list of names to convey enormity without obscuring individuality. A statue of a commander and his horse—or even a common soldier and his mates—may be more inspiring, but that is partly because of what is concealed when something is rendered symbolically rather than clerically. A complete list of names forces us to process death without elisions, conveying, as it has from the time of Athens, that, whatever has been won, we must remember longest all that has been lost.

 In 2004, Drew Gilpin Faust, now retired from the presidency of Harvard University, published a seminal article in *Civil War History* titled "'We Should Grow Too Fond of It': Why We Love the Civil War." The piece was a meditation on Robert E. Lee's offhand comment made to

James Longstreet as they watched in gleeful horror as the Confederate army mowed down wave after wave of bluecoats at Fredericksburg. "If war were not so terrible," Lee supposedly said, "we should grow too fond of it." Whether he said this or something like it is not important. What troubled Faust was not that two legendary figures fell momentarily in love with the war they were making but that, in retelling this story and others like it, academic historians induced the American public to fall in love with war generally. "In writing about war, even against war," Faust wondered, "do we nevertheless reinforce its attraction and affirm its meaning?" By imposing narrative discipline to the conflict, by treating the Civil War as a "moment of truth, as [an] occasion for decisive action, as [a] laboratory for agency—even for heroism," historians made the Civil War a more popular subject and, in the process, made war itself more likely and likable. Writing amidst the 2004 surge in Iraq, Faust had delivered one of the most devastating mea culpas in the history of the discipline.[31]

In 1991, the military banned photographers from taking pictures of the flag-draped coffins coming back to Dover Air Force Base. The Pentagon said the policy protected the dignity of the families. Many of the families said it protected Americans from facing the true cost of war. The policy remained in place for eighteen years, through the wars in Afghanistan and Iraq. Meanwhile an exhaustive study of the *New York Times*'s war coverage from World War I to the Iraq War shows that casualties were never a significant focus of the media. Casualties were rarely mentioned by name; in fact, they rarely made the front page. Only 11 percent of articles made even a fleeting acknowledgment that people were dying. Only 2 percent of articles reported "numerical details [paying] attention to the scale or rate of American losses." And none of this changed for a hundred years.[32]

Faust ended her 2004 mea culpa with a meditation on Susan Sontag's question: "Is there ... an antidote to the perennial seductiveness of war?" If there is, Faust thought, it could be found in the warning of the historian George Mosse: "We must never lose our horror, never try to integrate war and its consequences into our longing for the sacred. . . . [I]f we confront mass death naked, stripped of all myth, we may have slightly more chance to avoid making the devil's pact" with war. I agree with this, but I think there is also a way to combine the sacred and the horrible. Like the Athenians before us, we must count the dead as they did: as a list to be performed in song.[33]

# THREE

# ᵀHE POWER OF A NAME

*Challenging and highlighting abusive power dynamics
in our culture is my goal; replicating them is not.*

KARA WALKER

N March 1867, my hometown newspaper, the *Southern Watchman* (Athens, Georgia), published an unusual article dressing down its own readers. "We are pained to learn," groused the editor, John H. Christy, "that certain parties are very much 'disgruntled' because we used the word 'homicide' in speaking of the dead negro found in Mrs. King's horse lot." Four miles south of town, an unnamed freedman had been shot twice, once in the body and then in the head. Suspicion immediately fell upon a young white man from Kentucky who had drifted into the area, but authorities couldn't (or wouldn't) arrest him. When Christy dared lament that the man was getting away with "homicide," several of his readers had complained that the word did not apply, presumably because

they thought Black men were not men. For Christy, this was the last straw. For twenty-three years his politics had been *a little* less strident than those of his rivals at the Athens *Southern Banner*. He had been against immediate secession, for instance, and against the Confederate draft. Even so, for two decades he had defended slavery and the Confederate war effort—not least because he had enslaved a man named Lewis, whom he "affectionately" called "Old Tub," who turned the crank at the press.[1]

After the war, however, Christy found himself gradually more isolated as friends and neighbors gleefully embraced a policy of massive resistance to Reconstruction, which apparently condoned murder. "The fact that the negroes are now free does not justify any one in shooting them down," Christy explained in exasperation. "The law protects them in this respect as much as it ever did, and it always gave them just such protection against murder as it extended to the white race." The "dead negro" in Mrs. King's horse lot was not an isolated case. The week prior, another freedman in the same neighborhood had heard a noise in the night. "Who goes there?" he had asked. A pistol ball through the arm "was the only response he received." For all his support of the slave regime, Christy found himself confounded by a new world in which his Christian neighbors had managed to unrecognize murder. 'Homicide' "[is] the only word which an intelligent man could, under the circumstances, use with propriety," he said. "We employed that word just because it was the very identical word that suited our purposes." Unable to watch what Athens was becoming, Christy sold out his paper and moved away.[2]

A system in which some lives count and some lives don't produces so many injustices that it might seem silly to complain that it also produces bad data. But bad data has big consequences. In chapter 1, we discussed how and why good data—a "true count" of the dead—ultimately improved health outcomes for everyone.

In this chapter, we focus on how and why a true count of the murdered Black dead has proven particularly elusive in America.[3]

 Slavery, as it was practiced in the antebellum South, was deeply brutal but not entirely unmodern. Many of the innovations we associate with a mature capitalist economy—scientific management; vertical integration of supply chains; the evolution of commodification; accounting practices; property law; credit instruments; and technological solutions to specific productivity bottlenecks, including the scientization of beatings and insurance against "wastage" in the Middle Passage—all emerged with America's first big business: slavery. Whereas Karl Marx had placed enslaving in the most primitive stage of capitalism—the stage of conquest, enclosure movements, and precious metal extraction—recent historians present slavery as innovative, adaptable, and "modern."[4]

There are myriad problems with this approach. As we saw in chapter 1, the Slave Power—slaveholders who held political and economic influence in the South—fought fiercely the development of any data regime that might cast light on the enslaved population, even as statistics came of age, even as the sanitary progress of the whole human species came to depend on it. Instead, as data, the enslaved were most often treated as a strange species of property, especially by the "Big Data" project of the time: the antebellum census. The problem for slaveholders, however, was that if slaves were understood as property, they couldn't technically commit crimes. (No toaster has ever stood in the docket to answer for a robbery.) If slaveholders went the other way and treated the enslaved as persons of conscience before the law, they could make the enslaved answer for their crimes, but then the law might have to answer for any crimes against the enslaved.

In 1830, North Carolina Supreme Court justice Thomas Ruffin squared the legal circle for the South in the case of *State v.*

*Mann.* An enslaved woman named Lydia had been hired out to a poorer white man named John Mann. When Mann tried to lash her, Lydia ran, and Mann shot and wounded her. Mann was found guilty of battery and fined five dollars. Ruffin overruled. "The power of the master must be absolute to render the submission of the slave perfect," he said from the bench. The decision seemed to pain him. "I most freely confess my sense of the harshness of this proposition," he said. "As a principle of moral right every person in his retirement must repudiate it."[5]

Even after *Mann,* however, it remained technically illegal to murder the enslaved, though there were exceptions. "If the slave is in a state of insurrection," noted the great codifier of slave law T. R. R. Cobb, "the homicide is justifiable." "And if a slave is killed . . . at an unlawful assembly, combining to rebel," Cobb continued, all bets were off. Little protected enslaved women (and men) from rape, especially by their enslavers, as it was typically treated as criminal "trespass" against a piece of property. And nothing protected the enslaved from sale or even the most grotesque beatings. "Where the battery was committed by the master himself," Cobb said, "there would be no redress whatever, for the reason given in Exodus 21:21, 'for he is his money.'" With all this, however, the murder of the enslaved was illegal, full stop, and not just because they were valuable. In one of the few humane sentences Cobb wrote in his *Inquiry,* he noted that "the personal security of the slave being thus protected [from gratuitous murder] by express law, becomes *quasi* a right belonging to the slave as a person." Those who were enslaved, then, had one right as persons, exactly one more right than cows: they had, as Cobb put it, a quasi-human right not to be killed.[6]

At $3.5 billion, slaves were the single-most valuable commodity in America in 1860, dwarfing more than tenfold the value of all manufacturing infrastructure in the country. Between 1820 and 1860, the cotton crop doubled every decade, the 1860s crop being the largest and most profitable on record. And yes, Northerners made some of the money, but Southerners made more. With one-third of the country's white population, the South had two-thirds of the men worth over $100,000, men who would today be millionaires. The bigwigs of the South, noted one Alabamian at the time, "live in cotton houses and ride in cotton carriages. They buy cotton, sell cotton, think cotton, eat cotton, drink cotton, and dream cotton. They marry cotton wives, and unto them are born cotton children." Upton Sinclair famously noted that "it is difficult to get a man to understand something when his salary depends upon his not understanding it," and slaveholders' salaries depended deeply on disciplining (and overdisciplining) slaves and running them to the edge (or beyond) of endurance. A slave's legal right not to be killed, then, was something enslavers had incentive not to understand. What they most needed was a way of enforcing yet not enforcing their slaves' right to life, and the key to making it all work was the coroner's office.[7]

 The first formal mention we have of the coroner is in 1194 in the Articles of the Eyre. In medieval England, itinerant justices traveled the countryside along the Eyre (the judicial circuit), inspecting villages, holding court, settling disputes, and levying fines. This process was called "*holding* the pleas of the crown." By 1194, the process had become grossly inefficient and prone to abuse. Justices took years to complete their circuit, during which time villages were at the mercy of the county sheriff, who grew fat squeezing the peasants without kicking much up to the king. This was a particular problem for Richard I (Richard the Lionheart), who desperately needed money to finance his crusades, wars in France, and (once) his own ransom.

Enter Walter Hubert, legendary bureaucrat and architect of the 1194 articles, which, among other reforms, set up a new cadre of county officers tasked with *"keeping* the pleas of the crown" (*custos placitorum coronae*). The new coroners (or "crowners," as they were called for centuries) did not hold court but rather documented the claims the king could make when his court finally rolled into town. The duties of the new office were highly varied, but the charge was simple: generate revenue by promoting the king's rights and interests. When someone found buried treasure? It belonged to the king. When something of value washed ashore after a shipwreck? It belonged to the king. When someone stole from the royal fisheries? The coroner documented it and made sure not only that fines were paid but also that all such revenue made it to the royal treasury.

From the very beginning, coroners took particular interest in sudden deaths because they represented potential windfalls for the crown. Where the coroner suspected homicide or suicide, the crown could claim the perpetrator's estate. In the case of accidents, objects associated with the death could be seized and sold or given to the church as a deodand—an appeasement to God. Then there were the myriad petty fines. According to law, the "first finder" of a dead body was required to raise the "hue and cry," assemble a posse to hunt for suspects, and notify local officials, who in turn would notify the coroner. Meanwhile, the body had to rest undisturbed until the coroner arrived and could determine if the king could turn a profit in the Grim Reaper's wake. Every failure to follow protocol resulted in a fine (which incentivized peasants to drag bodies to different jurisdictions or hide them altogether). In such cases, the coroner fined the whole village. Thus, when a dead Norman was found on a village commons (which evidently happened a lot), the crowner levied a fine called the *murdrum*, from which the word *murder* derives.[8]

Gradually, a basic division of labor emerged between coroner and sheriff. The sheriff kept the peace among the living; the coroner kept the crown's pleas against the dead. Thus, the sheriff comes down to us through English literature as a local tyrant (think of the Sheriff of Nottingham in the Robin Hood mythos). And the coroner comes down to us as the representative of a distant, rapacious state. Thus in *Hamlet* does the gravedigger complain that a rich suicide has gotten a Christian burial because the "great folk" have paid off the crowner and are allowed to "drown or hang themselves" as they see fit. "Come, my spade," he concludes, the only *real* gentlemen are the "gardeners, ditchers, and grave-makers."[9]

By the time the coroner came to colonial America, his duties had stabilized around the investigation of untimely deaths. Colonial charters gave the power to appoint coroners to the governor or his council, though the office gradually became elective in certain states and districts. (The first election to the position of coroner was held in Plymouth Colony in 1636, but in most states, the position remained an appointed one well into the antebellum period.) In all states, the coroner was charged with convening an inquest when notified that someone in their jurisdiction (originally walking distance) had "come to his death by violence or suffered an untimely death." Such inquests, wherever practicable, were to take place "where the body lies" and were to be attended by a specific number of "good and lawful men" (eight in Massachusetts, fourteen in South Carolina) who were under oath to determine "upon a view of the body there lying dead, how, in what manner; and by whom he, or she, came to his or her death."[10]

Determining cause of death is so obviously a medical matter that it may seem strange that coroners typically had no medical training before the twentieth century. The questions aroused by any death go well beyond causation, however, and "untimely death" is especially fraught with implications—legal, religious, and financial. Where homicide is a suspected cause, the community demands justice and order from officials whose authority depends on the "peace and dignity" of the state. Where the

An 1826 cartoon captures the overlapping layers of intimacy and power embodied by the inquest. There is the authority of local landowners, the well-fed man by the fire; the authority of religion; the authority of the state, which has brought them all together; the authority of death itself, faced in cramped quarters; and the authority of local knowledge and common people, who note that the man isn't dead. The caption reads: "Juror: 'The man's alive, Sir, for he has open'd one eye.' Coroner: 'Sir, the doctor declar'd him Dead two hours since & he must remain Dead, Sir, so I shall proceed with the Inquest.'" Thos. McLean, *A Coroner's Inquest*, ca. 1826, etching, 18 × 23 in. London. *Courtesy of National Library of Medicine.*

deceased had property, assets are now loosed from their legal mooring, touching off waves of litigation (and, in the case of felonies, state seizures). Where the death is dramatic or gruesome, the press longs to feed upon and profit from the public's macabre taste. And then there are the spiritual dimensions: every death is a referendum on the life of the deceased and, to varying degrees, on life itself, and the authority of religion often rests on its ability to give meaning to seemingly meaningless death—to the sudden, the ghastly, and the tragic.

In nineteenth-century death investigation, medical certainty took a back seat to social considerations. When we think of our own police force, highway patrol, or FBI, we think of them as law enforcement—their job is to make sure everyone is obeying the law. But as historian Laura Edwards has shown, in the nineteenth century, authority had long arms, and the law had short ones. At the county level, where most Americans lived their lives, the job of the sheriff, coroner, and other magistrates was not to enforce the law but to "keep the peace"—the local understanding of the accepted social order.[11]

 In July 1824, an enslaved man named Edward escaped his enslaver, Alexander Matheson, owner of the general store on Camden, South Carolina's Courthouse Square. Edward fled south, making it as far as Stateburg before being recaptured and placed in the custody of one John Geno, who was charged with carrying him back to Camden via the Charleston Road. With two locks, a length of chain, and a bit of rope bought from the Stateburg general store, Geno lashed Edward's hands and chained him by the neck to the side of his horse and buggy. The distance they needed to cover was twenty-one miles, about a day's travel in the summer heat.[12]

Halfway through the trip, Edward began to tire. The morning was scorching, and his hands and feet were cramping. Geno said Edward was just being obstinate and so he hit him with his whip, giving, by his account, "but very few cuts and such as did no injury."

By two in the afternoon, the two men were three-quarters of the way to Camden when they stopped at a sluggish creek to rest and get a drink. The chain around Edward's neck was so tight, however, he could not swallow and instead staggered and fell over a log. Just at that moment the two men were overtaken by a stranger. Geno assured the man that Edward was shamming, and told Edward if he did not get up he would be dragged the rest of the way to town.

The stranger left, but two miles south of town, he was overtaken by Geno, now traveling alone. "What happened to the prisoner?" the stranger asked. Geno was vague: "He got to be so sullen [I] could do nothing with him. [I gave] him about 20 lashes at the log" and left him there.

Edward's death was horrific. All evidence suggests Geno made good on his threat to drag him to death. "The Jury found the body in one place," the coroner noted dryly, "the head in another, the underjaw in another & his clothes scattered every where [with] evidence apparent on the skeleton of his having received violence."

At the inquest, the jurors decided that only an animal could have done this much damage, and they clung to this notion even after the physician testified that "the severance of the head from the body would require great violence, more than would be probably exercised by hogs or dogs." Most of the jurors shrugged their shoulders and signed their names to their finding: "[the men assembled] do on their oaths say that they are of the opinion that the fellow Edward has come to his death by causes unknown to them."

One juror refused to sign, however. "How many murderers [must] be suffered to prowl in a community unpunished and unmolested?" asked an exasperated John Boykin Jr. To Boykin it was perfectly clear that Geno had "carried his threats into execution"; he had dragged Edward so long and so hard by the neck that the man had been decapitated and left for the animals. Boykin was a Camden lawyer, and his father was a South Carolina state legislator; he was absolutely loyal to the slave regime.

But was there really no limit to the depravities that a white man could visit upon the Black body? "It is murder," Boykin told his fellow jurors, and it was ridiculous to call it anything else.

I wish that Boykin's stance was typical. In the more than two thousand cases I've examined from South Carolina, his is the only "minority report" I've seen. More typical is a case in which all twelve members of a jury find that an enslaved woman had died of apoplexy after her daughter testified that her master had hit her mother with a shovel.

Why dwell upon such encounters? Doesn't it just reproduce all the indignities Blacks were forced to endure? No. The disciplinary violence of the slave regime belongs to its perpetrators alone. The only real question was, and remains, how we make the perpetrators answer for their crimes, and the key has always been data.

Take the case of an enslaved man named Ellick. On May 29, 1850, Ellick had been hired out to Thomas Mickle and stood seeding and hoeing in his field. Ellick had already worked a long hot day when Mickle approached on horseback to tell him that he would have to replant and re-hoe everything he had done. When Ellick protested that that would take all night, Mickle dismounted and threatened to flog him if he didn't return to his work. Ellick did so, but when Mickle rode off a little ways, Ellick suggested that it would probably be better for Mickle to hire somebody new to finish up. At this Mickle reared around and prepared to flog Ellick for his insolence.[13]

This basic pattern of escalation—the uneven clash of wills between the well-armed and the defenseless—replayed itself thousands of times across the antebellum South. Human beings have an enormous capacity for mental endurance, but for whatever reason, on this day Ellick snapped. Some combination of circumstances—some brewing for years, others existing only in the moment—made it impossible for him to stand down. When

Mickle moved to strike, Ellick said he wouldn't allow it. Mickle then pulled a gun, to which Ellick responded, "Shoot." At this, Mickle discharged a load of squirrel shot into Ellick's leg, but Ellick remained unfazed.

"You see you have shot me," Ellick said, but "I don't care for you[r] gun." Mickle then turned to report Ellick to his mistress (and presumably to get reinforcements or, one hopes, a doctor), but he hadn't gone far when he turned to see Ellick coming on the run. Mickle unloaded both barrels into Ellick's stomach. He was found by the jury to have acted in self-defense.[14]

Or take the case of an enslaved man named Peter. On June 15, 1838, Peter managed to wrest the stick he was being beaten with out of his overseer's hand and gave the man half a dozen good licks before he was subdued. Infuriated that he could not force Peter to submit to the lash, the overseer crushed Peter's head with a stone. In a similar case in May 1844, two overseers were so exasperated by an altercation with an enslaved man named Randal that they took turns lashing and resting until they had delivered more than four hundred blows. After his wounds were washed with salt to intensify the pain, Randal told them to go ahead and wash him with salt again—then he vomited and died.[15]

We know about these cases because they generated a legal record. Whatever the wishes of inquest juries who came back with cause of death "unknown," they set legal wheels in motion, and there is no statute of limitation on murder. The enslaved man Peter was stoned to death by Caleb Watkins. The enslaved man Randal was beaten to death by Alfred L. Hughes and Sebourn Randolph. All these men are dead. True justice may never be done, but justice never sleeps, and there is a final justice in naming names. "We cannot escape history," Abraham Lincoln said, and I would like to believe that he is right. I would like to believe that our actions "light us down, in honor or dishonor, to the latest generation." This, then, is our charge as historians. We are clerks in the reckoning. We keep the book. We light people down.[16]

Our problem as clerks is that we cannot know how many masters, overseers, drivers, and random whites killed in the breech of the Old South's "quasi law" against murder. The documentary record is too fragmented. We know only that the coroner was legally obligated to investigate every case. In her WPA interview, Mittie Freeman remembered the coroner as "that fellow that comes running fast when somebody gets killed." The coroner is mentioned in many of the most famous slave narratives, including those by Henry Box Brown and William Wells Brown. In his own *Narrative*, Frederick Douglass tells the story of an unnamed slave girl whose mistress "pounded in her skull" with a piece of firewood because she allowed the baby to wake the household. "I will not say that this murder most foul produced no sensation," Douglass later wrote. "It *did* produce a sensation. A warrant was issued for the arrest of Mrs. Hicks, but incredible to tell, for some reason or other, that warrant was never served, and she not only escaped condign punishment, but the pain and mortification as well of being arraigned before a court of justice." Frankly I find it fascinating that Douglass found the slave regime's failure to process an enslaved woman's murder "incredible to tell." But he was right about the coroner's office: there actually was a subtle game of community standards going on. Standing over the body of an enslaved person and surveying the grim damage, a coroner's jury was often perfectly comfortable recommending that a white be indicted and the enslaved be allowed to testify. The jury nullification came later, in the courtroom, when the mangled corpse was not actually present and the murderer was let off. By then the perpetrators had been held up to public scrutiny. Their judgment and decency had been questioned publicly and legally—but they hadn't been held to any real account.[17]

And this is the point: the essence of any counting system is its accountability; the essence of any "dis-counting" system is its corruptibility. In the antebellum South, the coroner acted as the bureaucratic pinch point in a death investigation process so deeply and purposely flawed that we have to squint to ascertain what was actually going on. The office functioned to screen slaveholders from any real accountability while also giving them the power to police their own and punish poor whites. What was needed was a set of bureaucrats from outside the South who could find a data regime that could penetrate the screen.[18]

 In *Inventing Human Rights*, Lynn Hunt describes the long process by which we, as humans, came to hold one another accountable for crimes against humanity itself. The process began (strangely) with novels—books that put us in the shoes and lives of people far removed from us in time, place, and circumstance. In 1761, Jean-Jacques Rousseau published his epistolary novel *Julie, or the New Heloise: Letters of Two Lovers Who Live in a Small Town at the Foot of the Alps.* The book was a runaway sensation across the Continent—not because many of its readers lived in small towns at the foot of the Alps but because it novelized *empathy*, creating an urgent demand that readers relate to characters whose experience was so dramatically different from their own. (Rousseau dedicated the book simply to the "subtleties of the [human] heart.")[19]

It is hard to overstate the power of this empathetic revolution, which preceded and made possible the political revolutions that produced the Declaration of Independence and the Declaration of the Rights of Man. Genetically, it is *not* true that we are designed to look out only for ourselves; we are designed by nature for amazing acts of self-sacrifice, though only in service of the genes that are most closely related to our own. Going beyond this—conceiving of a *human* family—only became possible when rising literacy rates and the steam-powered printing press flooded the world with stories that called upon us to identify with human *be-ing* itself. Growing up in Kentucky in the 1810s, Elizabeth Norris remembered: "We had few privileges & led very dull lives. We had no amusements to vary the monotony, no parties to bring us in contact with girls beyond our homes, and *worse than all* [emphasis mine] no books with charming little stories to excite noble impulses and stimulate us to acts of kindness and courtesy." For Norris, "charming little stories" became the bedrock of her empathy later in life, but her childhood without them had stymied her moral imagination.[20]

This rise of empathetic storytelling remade religion in the West. As historian Elizabeth B. Clark has noted, "Eighteenth-century sermons rarely used anecdotes drawn from secular life, relying instead on biblical parables to illustrate doctrinal points. By 1800 a new style of preaching had come into vogue: anecdotal rather than doctrinal, it embraced the moral value of human experience." The American pioneer of the new approach was Charles Grandison Finney, "the Father of Modern Revivalism," for whom selfishness was the original sin and empathy the key to salvation. Human beings weren't depraved and helpless, Finney said; they had only to "make a new heart," emptied of envy and filled with fraternal feeling. Where Jonathan Edwards had conjured the image of an angry God compelling obedience— "O sinner! . . . The God that holds you over the pit of hell, much as one holds a spider, or some loathsome insect over the fire, abhors you, and is dreadfully provoked"—Finney rebuilt religion on the God is love model. The result, said one witness, was "a new impulse" in America, a new drive "given to every philanthropic enterprise; the fountains of benevolence were opened, and men lived to *good*," where "good" was a verb—not a state of being but of doing on behalf of others.[21]

This new impulse collided very quickly with an old one— compelling Black people to labor—and it was a Finney disciple, Theodore Weld, who first unlocked the formula at the heart of this chapter: a modern human rights campaign is not just empathetic stories; it is empathy plus data. In 1839, Weld and his wife, Angelina Grimké, along with her sister, Sarah Grimké, produced *American Slavery as It Is: Testimony of a Thousand Witnesses*, a catalog of atrocities and an American call to conscience akin to Bartolomé de Las Casas's *Short Account of the Destruction of the Indies*. What made this book different from Las Casas's, however, was its emphasis on accountancy. As Weld noted, "Facts and testimonies are troops, weapons and victory, all in one."[22]

To compile the book, Angelina and her sister spent six months, six hours a day, combing through southern newspapers for runaway slave ads after noticing that a staggering proportion of the descriptions gave clear evidence that the runaways had been abused. Under headings like "Brandings, Maimings, & Gun-Shot Wounds" and "Mutilation of Teeth," the women compiled a devastating catalog of physical damage, giving only "the testimony of slaveholders themselves, to the mutilations, &c. by copying their own graphic descriptions of them, in advertisements published under their own names, and in newspapers published in the slave states." A typical ad might read: "Ranaway, a negro woman and two children; a few days before she went off, *I burnt her with a hot iron*, on the left side of her face, *I tried to make the letter M*." Another noted, "Ranaway a negro man named Henry, *his left eye out*, some scars from a *dirk* on and under his left arm, and *much scarred* with the whip." The ad for the "negro fellow Pompey, 40 years old" explained that he had been "*branded* on the *left jaw*."[23]

As historian Ellen Gruber Garvey has noted, *Slavery as It Is* was more than a book; it was a database, a revolution in information gathering and data conception. First, there was the sheer volume of the enterprise itself. Weld commuted every day from Fort Lee, New Jersey, to Manhattan, then the media center of America, and bought up every southern newspaper he could find, an estimated twenty thousand unique copies. Then the sisters began the careful process of grooming the information, sorting, cataloging, tagging, enumerating, indexing, and finding patterns. Finally, they weaponized and redeployed the information *as data*, which is to say facts that have been disciplined into a standardized form permitting easy analysis and cross-tabulation. With *Slavery as It Is*, Weld and the Grimkés did more than strike an anecdotal blow for abolition; they reconceived information itself, not as "the process of being informed" but as "a substance that could be morselized" and mined, cross-referenced, and put to living work. From an "undifferentiated pile of ads for runaway slaves, wherein dates and places were of primary importance," they created a biographical database that became the bedrock of the abolition movement. Harriet Beecher Stowe slept with *Slavery as It Is* "under her pillow at night till its facts crystallized into *Uncle Tom's Cabin*." "FACTS, FACTS, have set [everything] in motion," Angelina told her sister Anna. The Grimkés and Weld were among the first in the world to employ the term "human rights." More important, they were the first to base their human rights campaign on the modern formula—RESULTS = EMPATHY + DATA—penetrating the Slave Power's screen and helping to bring on a war.[24]

 In ways few historians have appreciated, the coroner's office remained the bureaucratic front line during Reconstruction. In Eric Foner's magisterial *Reconstruction: America's Unfinished Revolution*, the word "coroner" appears exactly zero times. The coroner's office is not meaningfully mentioned in Leon Litwack's *Been in the Storm So Long*, Steven Hahn's *A Nation under Our Feet*, David Blight's *Race and Reunion*, Gregory Downs's *After Appomattox*, or virtually any other landmark study of the South in the aftermath of the Civil War. And yet on July 9, 1876, the morning after a white mob sacked his town, Prince Rivers, the Black mayor of Hamburg, South Carolina, stood over the bodies of his slain citizens and convened a coroner's inquest. Because that is what you do the day *after* a massacre: You collect data. You name names. In the West, the inquest has always been the first link in the chain of justice because the official pronouncement of death sets all legal wheels in motion. In becoming "the Black Prince" and "the Power of Aiken County," Rivers had achieved something almost as precious as his freedom; he had achieved bureaucratic control. The inquest over, Rivers bundled together the pages of testimony and issued arrest warrants for eighty-seven white men, including Mathew Butler, future South Carolina senator, and Ben Tilman, future South Carolina governor. Notice of Rivers's inquest reverberated in newspapers throughout the North and was reprinted in the *New York Times*.[25]

For all this fanfare, however, the judicial process went no further because there were no Black or bureaucratic allies further up the chain. In the wake of the Hamburg Massacre, South Carolina's Republican governor begged the federal government for aid, but President Grant was noncommittal. "Now it will be a hundred years," Rivers told his son Joshua.

Just as an electrical circuit resists current to a greater or lesser degree (Ohm's law), a bureaucracy impedes or accelerates progress at every pinch point in the process. The Freedmen's Bureau papers, and especially the documents filed under "Murders and Outrages," paint a vivid portrait of federal agents astounded to discover that the Southern soldiers they had faced at Shiloh were as nothing compared to the Southern bureaucrats they faced in the aftermath. "The civil authorities are reported as not having taken any action in the matter," reported a bureau worker on the murder of freedman Ephraim McCallum by a white mob in Darlington. Such language was echoed in reports from across the state: "This case was laid before the civil authorities without effect" . . . "report of action not received" . . . "referred to civil authorities & not as yet heard from." In resisting occupation, guerrilla movements often exploit the bureaucratic bottlenecks in an enemy's process, and the county coroner's office had always been a place where state and federal law was adapted and interpreted to suit local circumstances.[26]

In his new book, *Murders and Outrages*, Bill Blair makes the case that the Freedmen's Bureau's efforts as a *documentary* body should be taken as seriously as its attempt to regulate labor contracts, open hospitals and schools, and distribute rations. Blair is the first scholar to take the full measure (complete with tables) of the bureau's attempt to document and deploy hard information about the reality of the violence that was visited upon Black communities in the wake of emancipation. As bureau workers and their legislative allies in Congress helplessly bore witness to racial injustice in the South, they instinctively and without training did what their abolitionist forebears had done before and what human rights workers now say is the first step in any truth and reconciliation campaign: They made a list. They named names. They aggregated evidence. They hoped this information would have value in their own time and hoped to convince Americans that Reconstruction was not anarchic, expensive, or doomed but a unique opportunity, lacking only a commitment from the federal government to provide enough resources (when they could have made a difference) to maintaining law and order on the ground. Ultimately, we know, the bureau's attempt to marshal information did not work, did not matter, became embroiled in politics, and was denied as "fake news."[27]

As Blair subtly shows, however, a well-kept death record is timeless because the data can always be put to living work. Bureau workers, helpless in their present, created an archive for the future and sent it to us, like a message in a bottle, across the century. Truth may be denied or ignored, but as long as it's *recorded*, all murder will out. In this sense, *Murders and Outrages* can be understood not merely as a history of Reconstruction but as a microhistory of information, a continuation of the human rights revolution begun under Weld and the Grimkés in *Slavery as It Is*.

 The case of Solomon George Washington Dill provides an excellent example of the delicacy of the bureau's position as a data collector. A native of Charleston, South Carolina, Dill had served as a private in the Confederate army before relocating to Kershaw County. There he proved a popular and rising politician—until, that is, he turned Republican. Representing Kershaw County at the 1868 South Carolina Constitutional Convention in January, Dill said that he hoped to build a new politics for the state, one that better represented the interests of South Carolina's long-suffering underclass, whether Black or white. "[I am often asked,] 'Mr. Dill, what are you doing in that damn n——r convention?'" Dill noted. "My reply was, 'I have always been a poor man, and always known to be on the side of the poor.'"[28]

The convention drew up a new constitution that conferred full suffrage and civil rights for Black Americans; that constitution was ratified by popular vote on April 6, 1868. This, then, was the foundation for Dill's new politics, and his home quickly became a hub to Kershaw County's Loyal Union League, a place where Kershaw's Black and white population mingled freely. This social interaction, as much as the political action itself, galled Kershaw's white minority, and in his campaign for county commissioner Dill became the target of almost daily death threats. "Our men put old Lincoln up Shit creek," Emanuel Parker was heard to say on May 15, "and we'll put old Dill up." On May 22, a local white man, Abraham Rabon, met a Dill supporter in the street who told him he was "going down to Mr. Dill's to hear a speech." "Yes, you are all going to hell as fast as you can," Rabon retorted. And "that damned [Dill] will be knocked into a cocked hat before many days." William Kelly was overheard on multiple occasions threatening Dill's life. Quarrelsome and (likely) intoxicated, he got into a shouting match with a Dill supporter on the public square in Camden. "Yes, by God! you all take old Dill for your god," Kelly yelled, "and God damn him! I'll kill him." When he heard that Dill was elected, Kelly said simply, "If it is the last thing I do, I'll kill Dill."[29]

In justifying their threats of violence, men like Kelly appalled themselves and their friends with stories that Dill was preaching violence among the Black population, telling crowds that if he were killed, "the freed people must rise and avenge him, and kill from the cradle up, for 20 miles square." This specific language, "from the cradle up"—an allusion to Nat Turner and a war of racial extinction—became so stuck in the minority white mind that it was still being reported as fact in local histories well into the twentieth century. Witnesses who actually heard him speak, however, say that Dill preached a political gospel of self-help, patience, forbearance, and peace.[30]

At sunset on June 4, William Kelly and his brother met at the home of Emanuel Parker, where they purchased two bottles of whiskey and rendezvoused with other conspirators. They then proceeded under cover of darkness to Dill's home. The election over, Dill appears to have let his guard down. Though his life had been threatened many times, he may not have expected that they would go through with it. Perhaps, as some of his supporters would later say, he "expected to be killed, but that so long as he lived he would stand firmly to his avowed political principles because he believed them to be just to all men." Regardless, the house was poorly defended. Nestor Ellison, an older Black man and by some accounts infirm, nevertheless insisted on serving as Dill's bodyguard and was the only one on watch. At the sound of whispers outside the house, Ellison rose from his chair and opened the door to investigate. He was shot in the head. Simultaneously Dill was fired upon through a window, the bullet crashing into "the cervical portion of the spine." The mob now opened fire on the house generally, perhaps ten rounds in all. Rebecca Dill was shot in the leg. Her guest, Nancy Burnett, ran out of the house to beg for the lives of her three children who were still inside. From the darkness an exultant voice answered, "By God, I've got all I want," and the mob withdrew.[31]

Dill's was one of the first major political assassinations in Reconstruction-era South Carolina. The question for the Loyal Union League, the Freedmen's Bureau, and the Union army was what to do about it; eyes were watching, and precedents would be set. Assigned to investigate Dill's case—and to ensure that *something* happened—was 1st Lt. George Frederic Price, Fifth U.S. Cavalry, and assistant to the judge advocate for the Second Military District (North and South Carolina).

Price had been born in 1835 in Newburgh, New York, a town situated seventy miles up the Hudson River from Manhattan and made somewhat famous as the site of the Newburgh Conspiracy, the almost mutiny of the Continental army that George Washington had stared down in 1783. At the outbreak of the Civil War, Price had been in California, and he joined the Second California Cavalry Regiment, remaining a career cavalry officer after the war until he was "severely wounded in a fight with the Sioux" in 1876.[32]

In his regimental history, *Across the Continent with the Fifth Cavalry*, Price gave spare attention to his South Carolina years, partly because they were so unlike everything else he had done in his career. In an operational sense, fighting rebels and fighting Sioux had been what he was trained to do. By contrast, "the duties devolved upon [us]" in Reconstruction, Price noted, were "in many respects foreign to the profession of arms." The occupying U.S. troops were in a delicate position, needing to "win the hearty commendations of the citizens" even as they compelled them to obey the law.[33]

To Price, it was perfectly clear that "the killing of Mr. Dill was a political assassination. This fact stands out in bold relief and is beyond dispute." The question was how to compel the civil authority to act. "I am assured by a member of the coroner's jury that the whites on it scarcely looked at the dead bodies," Price reported to his superiors, and "did not appear to have any desire to ascertain the locality of the wounds thereon, and that a general indifference was manifested. The inquest appears to have been hurried through as speedily as possible."[34]

In the absence of a civil investigation, Price determined to conduct one of his own. Aided by the bureau agent stationed at Camden and two detectives assigned by the provost marshal's office, Price and his team gathered a mountain of circumstantial evidence, especially from local Black citizens. "The blacks have given me all the assistance in their power," Price noted, "and have uniformly exhibited good conduct under circumstances well calculated to arouse their worst passions, for Dill was their trusted and proved friend." The local whites were another matter. "While the community professes to denounce this assassination," Price said, "no white citizen . . . (excepting Judge W. G. Leitner) has approached me with any information." Price was somewhat confounded by this. He knew that many of the whites living in Camden's Kirkwood suburbs "viewed with disfavor the measures devised by Congress for the reorganization of the governments of the States lately in rebellion." But surely it crossed the line of Christian decency to gun down a neighbor in his own home in front of his wife and child over a political disagreement. "My associations with the citizens of Kershaw district have been heretofore pleasant," Price confided to his superiors. "They are now pleasant; and I regret that the circumstances surrounding the assassination of Dill compel me to say that I am convinced that the neighbors of Dill can, if they choose to do so, give information which would lead to the arrest and conviction of every person engaged in his assassination."[35]

Ultimately Price and his team went around the civil authorities one last time to make their own arrests, sending twenty alleged conspirators to the Citadel in Charleston. These men were questioned, but Price probably wasn't expecting them to implicate themselves. Rather, he hoped that by sending them away he could convince some of the local whites with firsthand knowledge of the crime to come forward without fear of reprisal. When they failed to do so, Price's case fell apart, and with it, his hopes for Reconstruction. In the end, he decided, the problem wasn't the assassins. It was the "pleasant" people. "It is my belief," he wrote in his final report, "that when all the truth becomes known in regard to this assassination, the parties committing the crime, together with the accessories before and after the fact, will be counted by scores." A minority of whites were willing to kill their own neighbor. A majority were willing to look the other way. Price was neither the first nor the last to find such a situation hopeless. In the fall, he learned that the fifth cavalry was moving out. "The rank and file of the regiment," he wrote in his memoir, "were well pleased when [reassigned] to the western frontier of Kansas for service against the hostile Indians of the Plains."[36]

There is a reason the position of coroner was among the first Black Americans held in Reconstruction and one of the last they relinquished. Yes, it was one of the lowest rungs on the ladder of elected service, but it was also the front line in the battle for something that really mattered: bureaucratic control.

 Human rights are timeless. It actually doesn't matter whether abuses were committed in the distant past or yesterday. If data exists, as historians, we tabulate it, just as our forebears did, because we have to believe that the truth will out. This sense—that in accountancy there is accountability—has become a cornerstone of human rights scholarship. As geographer Amy J. Ross argues in "The Body Counts," the first step after any genocide or human rights violation is simply to name the dead. "Establishing the identities of the killed, and the killers, is crucial," she notes. Mass human catastrophe invites general reactions of revulsion and righteousness when what is needed first and foremost is accuracy. Only when we count and categorize the dead, Ross notes, can we "address the ways in which [the] violence [should be] understood as either acts of war or crimes of war." The Human Rights Data Analysis Group has come to the same conclusion. "We believe truth leads to accountability [and] accountability hinges on truth," the organizers note. "To this end, we apply statistical and scientific methods in the analysis of human rights data so that our partners—human rights advocates—can build scientifically defensible, evidence-based arguments that will result in outcomes of accountability."[37]

While it is entirely too late to achieve actual justice for the many Black people who were terrorized during the era of slavery and "redemption," it is not too late to give a better accounting of those who gave their lives. This is no less than we do for the mass graves we find in Iraq or Mexico, and it is what scholars of social justice suggest is the first step in reckoning and reconciliation after any war: you count the dead.

In 2016 I launched the website CSI: Dixie, a project devoted to the simple premise that every society must answer for its morgue. Collecting thousands of coroners' inquests from across the antebellum South, the site lays bare the staggering brutality of the slave regime. Even before unsympathetic coroners and juries, enslaved men, women, and children were found to have died variously of "cruel treatment," "excessive driving," "too many strokes of the whip," and every possible variation of being beaten: "beaten with a cowhide," "beaten with [a] club," "beaten with a . . . fence rail," or simply "beaten to death." I embarked on the project because of my strong belief that all murder will out if all murders are recorded, but the project quickly took a psychological toll. As the names multiplied and the list got longer, the whole experience seemed somehow reminiscent of waiting to see whose name would join Eric Garner, Michael Brown, Tamir Rice, Walter

Scott, Freddie Gray, Alton Sterling, Philando Castile . . . and now Breonna Taylor and George Floyd . . . and now Daunte Wright . . .

But the very point of being a bureaucrat—a clerk of the reckoning—is that there can be no fatigue. Whenever I get down, I try to remember Emerson and his ilk's opinion of the tireless Shattuck: "Whoso wisheth to do scientific penance, let him read 100 pages of his figures."

Research shows that in any mass tragedy there is for most of us a diminution of relative sympathy with each next victim. All of us can identify with a single tragedy—Elián González becomes the face of the Cuban "boat people"; Terri Schiavo focuses our conversation on right-to-die issues; Omran Daqneesh, the ash-covered toddler from Aleppo, brings home to us the steep cost of the Syrian conflict. But if Omran had had a brother or a sister? (In fact, he has both, but they were metaphorically and literally cropped out of the photo because for almost all of us, as the number of victims rises, our sympathy curdles into titillation, horror, and indifference.) The phenomenon is so commonplace that it has been said a thousand times without ever being deeply understood. The most chilling encapsulation is (mis)attributed to Stalin: "The death of one man is a tragedy. The deaths of millions are a statistic." But we even put such words into the mouth of an alien seeking to define the essential aspect of our species: "I've noticed that about your people," says Mr. Spock to Dr. McCoy. "You find it easier to understand the death of one than the death of a million. You speak of the objective hardness of the Vulcan heart—yet how little room there seems to be in yours."[38]

The latest research suggests that this collective apathy in the face of mass tragedy turns out to be as much a failure of numeracy as morality. "I am deeply moved if I see one man suffering and would risk my life for him," noted the biochemist Albert Szent-Györgyi, and yet "I [can] talk impersonally about the possible pulverization of our big cities, with a hundred million dead. I am unable to multiply one man's suffering by a hundred million."

Numbers are also key to a related psychological phenomenon, "bystander apathy," which notes that our tendency to intervene in an immediate and unfolding tragedy declines in proportion to the number of people available to help.[39]

Think about what this means: The larger and more diffuse the tragedy, the less likely we are to respond. The more of us who are available to help, the less likely we are to do anything. This is why the "math of after," the "power of a name," and the impulse to sit amidst a human disaster and make a list are so important. When catastrophe strikes, it is our systems, not our consciences, that are likely to save us, because it is as much a problem of numeracy, not morality, that prevents us from truly understanding the catastrophe in the first place.

Counting the dead only matters, however, if you make the dead count. It has always been a two-step process. On Juneteenth 2020, after advocating for three decades for better use-of-force statistics, criminology professor Geoffrey Alpert sounded as exasperated as Lemuel Shattuck in testifying at a Presidential Commission on Law Enforcement: "It's always been obvious," Alpert told the panel, "if we don't know the data, how do we identify the problem? The only way forward is with evidence, but we continue to spin in circles." The spinning is deliberate, as Alpert knew—as Shattuck knew 170 years before.[40]

The Federal Bureau of Investigation began its Uniform Crime Reporting program in 1929 and quickly became the nation's clearinghouse for crime statistics. The original criminal categories deemed worthy of national collection were murder, manslaughter, rape, aggravated assault, larceny, and stolen vehicles. Arson was added in 1979. The LEOKA database (Law Enforcement Officers Killed and Assaulted) was added in 1996. Not until 2015 was a task force formed to discuss the possibility of collecting data on use of force in a country where three Americans per day are killed by police. Only in 2019 did the project start collecting data, and even then, law enforcement agencies were encouraged but not required to participate.[41]

In 2015, in the absence of national leadership, communities of color exposed what white data collectors had been trying to hide and what Black communities have known instinctively for a century: Black Americans are two and a half times more likely to be killed by police, and twice as likely to be killed by police while unarmed. Comprising just 13 percent of the population, they are 33 percent of the unarmed victims of fatal police shootings. Staggeringly, nine out of ten off-duty police officers who are killed by police are Black or Latino.[42]

We've counted the dead. It is time to make them count.

# EPILOGUE

# THE TEMPLE OF TIME

*Death is not the opposite of life but a part of it.*

HARUKI MURAKAMI

HIS book has made three reinforcing arguments: If we count the dead, we might have better public health. If we count the dead, we might make fewer or "better" wars. If we count the dead, we might strike stronger blows for social justice. To this list, I will add one other:

## IF WE COUNT THE DEAD, WE MIGHT WRITE BETTER HISTORY

All that we are, we are because we die. Without death, we would not exist biologically, culturally, or historically. We have death to thank for everything.

For millions of years, life that was maladapted to its ecological niche died. Life that was well-adapted died also, giving birth and giving way to a next generation that might be better adapted still. Nature is an endless struggle to stay one step ahead of predators and parasites that are evolving also, and death makes the whole thing work. Darwin's "survival of the fittest" guided our development as a species from a single cell in a septic ocean to an erect monkey playing with fire. In the process, nature invented cool things: a hawk's eyeball or frogs that can freeze and recover or bury themselves for years beneath a desert in a shell of hardened mucus until the rain comes. But nature never invented immortality. And that is because Mother Nature's first and most important invention, the foundation on which all else rests, is death. Death is nature's battery, its engine, its churn.[1]

Death is the foundation of human culture. When our primitive ancestors closed their eyes to sleep, they did not cease to be forever—they slipped into a disembodied world. Logically they concluded that when they closed their eyes for forever, the noncorporeal part of them would live on in some form, navigating an endless dreamscape of peril and possibility. Preparing for what they thought would be a forever afterlife, they created religion, Stonehenge, the Great Pyramid, Cahokia, and culture itself. Culture's essential function is to pass from one generation to the next something of what has been learned or built—and a huge part of that culture is the meaning we make in the face of our known mortality. The funeral was one of our earliest cultural rites; grave goods were among our first cultural artifacts. In rituals as old as humankind, we gave the dead our things because, wherever they were going, we would go there soon.[2]

And then we told stories about them—the foundation of history itself. History reeks of death, and I do not mean merely that wars, murders, and assassinations are the stuff of good history, though there is some truth to that. "What would there be in a story of happiness?" noted the great French thinker André Gide. "Only what prepares it, only what destroys it can be told." Death makes history possible in the same way that it makes life possible—by making change possible. Historians do not specialize in old things because they are old. That's an antiquarian. Historians specialize in old things because they hope to understand how the old became new; change over time is the sine qua non of what it means to be a historian, and there would be no change, no historical evolution, no epochs or ages, without death.[3]

And yet as Americans, we have created a largely death-denying culture. We quarantine death behind a gauzy hospital curtain. We hope we don't catch it because it is ugly and embarrassing and implicates us a little, not least because it reminds us of our own mortality. So we happily outsource the care of our dying to strangers to whom we throw fortunes hoping they will heroically prolong the inevitable. It was not always thus. For generations, we died in our sick beds and living rooms, surrounded by our family. Relatively recently, we decided that the dead did not, for their own undead sake, need to be venerated or exorcised or appeased with our stuff. The exceptional among them could live as legend; the familiar among them could live in our personal memory. But after the Enlightenment, we banished the haints and the haunts and the spirits in the stone. "To the dead we owe only the truth," said Voltaire. "The Earth belongs to the living," said Jefferson.[4]

This book has been dedicated to the work the dead have done, continue to do, and might yet do, as data. Students in my Death: A Human History class think I'm a little morbid because I write about death all the time. To me, thinking about the dead is like lying in the grass and staring at the stars. The vastness of the night sky should crush us with the gravity of our own insignificance. Instead, we feel privileged to encompass such vastness in our own humble eye. So it is with history; our smallness before time somehow amplifies the connection we feel to something so much larger than ourselves. John Keats had this same sensation when he came home from a particularly good party: "Myself [does not go] home to myself," he said, "but the identity of everyone in the room begins so to press upon me, that I am in a very little annihilated." We study history to be multiplied. We study history to be annihilated and then to be remade—better, stronger, more forgiving, more thankful. Above all, more thankful—for the men and women who suffered so much and sacrificed so much so that we could all live such lucky, miraculous lives.[5]

Certainly we study history because it has enormous social utility. Inspiring and appalling us by turns, history serves as a collective reminder of all that we need to live up to and all that we need to live down.

Certainly we study history because it has enormous philosophical utility. Since the days of Homer and Herodotus, history has been one long meditation on human nature. The "real subject" of history, said the legendary French historian Numa Fustel de Coulanges, "is the human spirit." This does not mean that history has been an aspirational tale of advancement. History is mostly bad news—a vast tapestry of taking and getting taken. But you cannot be free of a thing if you don't know that you're ensnared. The novelist Michael Crichton reportedly said, "If you don't know history, then you don't know anything. You are a leaf that doesn't know it is part of a tree." And two hundred years earlier, Sir John Dalberg-Acton told students at Cambridge, "If the Past has been an obstacle and a burden, knowledge of the Past is the safest and the surest emancipation."[6]

Mostly, though, we study history because we like to watch people take their turn on earth until they are buried under it. The profoundest lesson I ever learned as a historian I learned from a dog-eared 1978 translation of *The Song of Roland*. As the translator Frederick Goldin explained in the introduction, the past, by its past-ness, has an "urge" to be epic. Roland, we know, is going to die. We know, when he dons his armor, that he has done it for the last time. We know that he can't *not* go into battle because he has already gone. Betrayed and defeated, Roland lifts the oliphant to his lips and blows until his temples burst because he is trapped in his own literary and historical inevitability. "Roland is the agent of an accomplished action," Goldin notes, "and we are privileged to witness [his] graceful conformity to the rule of necessity."[7]

History is my religion; the archive, my church; research, my sacrament (and my penance). I never feel so alive as when I am entombed with my dead in some archival catacombs, convinced I am searching for their humanity, knowing I am searching for my own. To be an archive rat, said Derrida, "is to burn with a passion. It is never to rest, interminably, from searching for the archive, right where it slips away. It is to run after the archive, even if there's too much of it. . . . It is to have a compulsive, repetitive . . . irrepressible desire to return to the origin, a homesickness, a nostalgia for . . . the most archaic place of absolute commencement." As historians, the archive is our psychic headwaters. For narrow professional reasons, we go to answer research questions, but we know the pilgrimage runs deeper. Like time-tripping flaneurs, we watch the dead live their lives, not as we live ours, and we revel in the differences, inspired by all that we have to live up to, ashamed of all that we need to live down. This encounter, Carolyn Steedman tells us, is physical. The dead press their concerns upon us, and we come away with their dust in our lungs.[8]

Somehow these metaphysical rites coexist with our rising interrogation of the process by which our great archives were built. (We love our god, but we doubt our god, too.) The "archival turn" that produced this skepticism is relatively old now. Derrida first published *Archive Fever* in 1995. Ann Stoler's "Colonial Archives and the Arts of Governance" came out in 2002, the same year as Steedman's *Dust*. Summarizing the general line of thought—that archives encode and enshrine power—Stoler noted, "Scholars need to move from archive-as-source to archive-as-subject. . . . [We need to] view archives not as sites of knowledge retrieval, but of knowledge production . . . [as] cultural agents of 'fact' production [and] state authority." While this thinking may be twenty-plus years old, there are reasons to believe that we are in the middle and not the end of that turn. As the country has lurched to the dystopian right, the urge to interrogate inherited structures, especially structures of information, has deepened. Every generation takes on inequality, and each finds it rooted deeper than they originally thought. At least since Gayatri Spivak's "Can the Subaltern Speak?" (1985), there has been a debate over whether the archive really can be read "against the grain" of the forces that created it. And yet the dead still speak to us, even from their flawed tombs. Very gradually, from out of the shadows of colonial administrators, enslavers, and great men, a people's history emerged.[9]

While historians are neither quants nor bureaucrats, we—like them—are death watchers. Like the coroner and the mortality census marshal before us, we are wholesalers in mortality, registering all who have gone before, struggling to make meaning and bring order to an aggregation of sad things that happened to other people who are no longer here. As for the coroner and the mortality census marshal, the debate over "who counts?" has had a profound impact on the historical profession. In the early nineteenth century, history was told in the "great man" model; only the most exceptional human beings effectively counted, and the lives of the many were subsumed in the lives of the few. Gradually the discipline of history, like the other death-counting disciplines examined here, became more exhaustive and inclusive. Long before cliometrics or the social scientization of their discipline, historians began to grapple with the idea that the mass of men and, ultimately, women, make history, too.[10]

In 1849, Emma Willard published her *Willard's Historic Guide: Guide to the Temple of Time; and Universal History for Schools.* Willard had founded the first institution of higher learning for women in Troy, New York, in 1821. "We too are primary existences," she said of her sisters, and "not the satellites of men." And yet she, too, had been captured by the idea that "history is

Emma Willard's *Temple of Time* was at once a breakthrough in data visualization and a reification of the "great man theory" of history. Emma Willard, *The Temple of Time* (New York: A. S. Barnes, 1846). Courtesy of David Rumsey Historical Map Collection.

made up of the lives of eminent men." Her *Temple of Time* is a staggering break-through in informatics. All of human history, as then conceived, was rendered as a sort of memory palace: the pillars were kings and heads of state. The floor was tiled with the major events that occurred in their reign. The ceiling was vaulted with the "best of what has been thought and said"—the philosophers, poets, and painters who made timeless things in their limited time. "In a small space," wrote a reviewer, Willard had "marshalled the master spirits who have swayed the actions of the masses" and reduced them to "simplicity, unity, and order." The result was an "inner temple" where all Americans should seek to dwell.[11]

But human life is no palace. Our poets, prophets, and artists are not propped up by our statesmen. Willard, like anyone, had made assumptions about how time works, how power works, and how human history proceeds. Time, we know—in ways Willard couldn't—is not linear. Darwin was wrong: change does not occur gradually. It occurs by punctuated equilibria: long periods of stasis are shattered by periods of dramatic change. And in sponsoring and resisting change, our governments are never perfect. Making laws and wars, they dominate and compel and are too often captured by special interests and put to selfish ends. But governments are also the mode by which we combat common enemies for the common good. The result is at best staggered progress. Government policies leech the niacin out of our corn and put it in our bread. As the embodiment of our collective inequalities and interests, fears and failings, hopes and dreams, the "state" is neither angel nor devil, and can be turned to ends foul or fair by the wisdom or depravity of the people. What the people most need, then, is to focus on, have faith in, and act upon "good data." Just as archives (and their inequalities) reproduce themselves in our history, data regimes (and their inadequacy) reproduce themselves in our policies.[12]

This book has been dedicated to the moment when we first counted our dead, how we gradually and grudgingly got better at it, and why the consequences proved so vast and important. At the core of the argument is the simple observation that human outcomes improved dramatically when we first applied the dictum that now animates humanitarian causes worldwide: count the dead and make them count. Making cholera answer for its "crimes" against humanity turns out to be not so very different from making Stalin or law enforcement answer for theirs. In all cases, you begin with an overriding sense, at once clerical and moral, that in accountancy there is accountability, that in records there is a reckoning, that RESULTS = EMPATHY + DATA, and that until we count the dead, we can never make them count. In the end, it's actually quite simple: Every body has to matter, every body has to count—because when every body matters, everybody matters. When every body counts, everybody counts. The critical public health and social justice questions turn out to be one and the same. Who dies of what, where, when, and why turns out to be the most compelling questions in the world—and the ones most likely to save our lives.

# NOTES

*Preface*

1. Uta C. Merzbach and Carl B. Boyer, *A History of Mathematics* (New York: John Wiley & Sons, 2011); Charles Seife, *Zero: The Biography of a Dangerous Idea* (New York: Viking, 2000).

2. Caroline Shenton, *The Day Parliament Burned Down* (New York: Oxford University Press, 2012).

3. J. D. B. De Bow, *Mortality Statistics of the Seventh Census of the United States, 1850* (Washington: A.O.P. Nicholson, 1855), 5; Machiavelli, *The Prince* (London: Grant Richards, 1903), 66–67.

4. The history of death begins with Phillipe Ariès, *The Hour of Our Death: The Classic History of Western Attitudes toward Death over the Last One Thousand Years* (New York: Knopf, 1981). Before Ariès, death, like childhood, seemed universal and beyond historicization. Other critical early texts in historical death studies include Ivan Ilych, *Medical Nemesis* (Toronto: Bantam, 1976); Ernest Becker, *The Denial of Death* (New York: Free Press, 1973). For death history in early America, see Margaret M. Coffin, *Death in Early America: The History and Folklore of Customs and Superstitions of Early Medicine, Funerals, Burials, and Mourning* (Nashville, TN: Nelson, 1976); Nancy Isenberg and Andrew Burstein, *Mortal Remains: Death in Early America* (Philadelphia: University of Pennsylvania Press, 2002); *The Sacred Remains: American Attitudes toward Death, 1799–1883* (New Haven, CT: Yale University Press, 1996); James Farrell, *Inventing the American Way of Death, 1830–1920* (Philadelphia: Temple University Press, 1980); Lewis O. Saum, "Death in the Popular Mind of Pre–Civil War America," in *Death in America,* ed. David Stannard (Philadelphia: University of Pennsylvania Press, 1974); Martha V. Pike and Janice Gray Armstrong, eds., *A Time to Mourn: Expressions of Grief in Nineteenth Century America* (Stony Brook: Museums

at Stony Brook, 1980); Russ Castronovo, *Necro Citizenship: Death, Eroticism, and the Public Sphere in the Nineteenth-Century United States* (Durham, NC: Duke University Press, 2001); Robert V. Wells, *Facing the "King of Terrors": Death and Society in an American Community, 1750–1990* (Cambridge: Cambridge University Press, 2000); Erik R. Seeman, *Death in the New World: Cross-Cultural Encounters, 1492–1800* (Philadelphia: University of Pennsylvania Press, 2011).

5. Lawrence B. Goodheart, *Abolitionist, Actuary, Atheist: Elizur Wright and the Reform Impulse* (Kent: Kent State University Press, 1990), 145. On the standardization of death classification in America, see Halbert L. Dunn, "The Evaluation of the Effect upon Mortality Statistics of the Selection of the Primary Cause of Death," *Journal of the American Statistical Association* 31, no. 193 (March 1936): 112–23; Jeffrey K. Beemer, "Diagnostic Prescriptions: Shifting Boundaries of Nineteenth-Century Disease and Cause-of-Death Classification," *Social Science History* 33, no. 3 (Fall 2009): 307–40; Douglas L. Anderton and Susan Hautaniemi Leonard, "Grammars of Death: An Analysis of Nineteenth-Century Literal Causes of Death from the Age of Miasmas to Germ Theory," *Social Science History* 28, no. 1 (Spring 2004): 111–43.

6. Published every two years, the World Wildlife Fund's *Living Planet Report, 2020* reports that "the population sizes of mammals, birds, fish, amphibians and reptiles have seen an alarming average drop of 68% since 1970." "The findings are clear: Our relationship with nature is broken," https://livingplanet.panda.org/en-us. For the full report, see Rosamunde Almond, Monique Grooten, and Tanya Petersen, eds., *Living Planet Report, 2020: Bending the Curve of Biodiversity Loss* (Gland, Switzerland: WWF, 2020), https://f.hubspotusercontent20.net/hubfs/4783129/LPR/PDFs/ENGLISH-FULL.pdf. See also Nathan Pacoureau, Cassandra L. Rigby, Pete M. Kyne, et al., "Half a Century of Global Decline in Oceanic Sharks and Rays," *Nature* 589 (January 2021): 567–71; John R. Platt, "What We've Lost: The Species Declared Extinct in 2020," *Scientific American*, January 13, 2021.

7. James C. Scott, *Seeing Like a State: How Certain Schemes to Improve the Human Condition Have Failed* (New Haven, CT: Yale University Press, 1999); James Gleick, *The Information: A History, a Theory, a Flood* (New York: Vintage, 2012).

8. Alan Hunt and Gary Wickham, *Foucault and Law: Towards a Sociology of Law as Governance* (London: Pluto Press, 1994), 76.

9. Michael C. Behrent, "Accidents Happen: François Ewald, the 'Antirevolutionary' Foucault, and the Intellectual Politics of the French Welfare State," *Journal of Modern History* 82, no. 3 (September 2010): 587.

In fairness, there was always a flexibility to Foucault's understanding of power-knowledge. Especially in *The History of Sexuality* he describes how power both depends on knowledge and reproduces itself in our knowledge, at once constraining what we can think and do but also opening up new ways of conceiving of ourselves. For more on Ewald, see Behrent, "Accidents Happen," 585–624. See also Beatrix Hoffman, "Scientific Racism, Insurance, and Opposition to the Welfare State: Frederick L. Hoffman's Transatlantic Journey," *Journal of the Gilded Age and Progressive Era* 2, no. 2 (April 2003): 150–90.

10. See James Ciment, "Life Expectancy of Russian Men Falls to 58," *British Medical Journal* 319, no. 7208 (1999): 468.

11. As humans, we have never died equally, and from hurricanes to pandemics, disasters tend to fall hardest on the most vulnerable. In the contemporary United States, for instance, Black people make up a disproportionate share of COVID-19 cases and deaths due to their inferior living conditions, reduced access to health insurance and health care, underlying medical conditions, and jobs that require them to work in person. What is relatively new, however, is the self-decimation of the white population. Today, the white suicide rate is twice that of the rate for Black people. This may have something to do with perceived status declension in a country rapidly become majority minority, but the bigger contributor is the policies that are enacted as "solutions" to that erroneous belief. Limiting immigration, for instance, only ensures that the aging white population will have fewer younger workers to take care of them and pay their benefits. "When white backlash policies became laws," Jonathan Metzl notes in *Dying of Whiteness*, "as in cutting away health care programs and infrastructure spending, blocking expansion of health care delivery systems, defunding opiate-addiction centers, spewing toxins into the air, or enabling guns in public spaces, the result was—and I say this with the support of statistics detailed in the chapters that follow—increasing rates of death." See Jonathan M. Metzl, *Dying of Whiteness: How the Politics of Racial Resentment Is Killing America's Heartland* (New York: Basic Books, 2020), 8. See also Anne Case and Angus Deaton, *Deaths of Despair and the Future of Capitalism* (Princeton, NJ: Princeton University Press, 2020).

12. On the history of numeracy, certainty, and statistics, see Tore Fangsmyr, J. L. Heilbron, and Robin E. Rider, eds., *The Quantifying Spirit in the Eighteenth Century* (Berkeley: University of California Press, 1990); Patricia Cline Cohen, *A Calculating People: The Spread of Numeracy in Early America* (Oxfordshire: Routledge, 1999); Theodore M. Porter, *The Rise of Statistical Thinking, 1820–1900* (Princeton, NJ: Princeton University Press,

1988); Theodore M. Porter, *Trust in Numbers: The Pursuit of Objectivity in Science and Public Life* (Princeton, NJ: Princeton University Press, 1996). On the related history of data visualization, see especially Johanna Drucker, *Graphesis: Visual Forms of Knowledge Production* (Cambridge, MA: Harvard University Press, 2014); Murray Dick, *The Infographic: A History of Data Graphics in News and Communications* (Cambridge, MA: MIT Press, 2020). On the history of information more generally, see James Gleick, *The Information: A History, a Theory, a Flood* (New York: Pantheon, 2011). On the specific history of human beings as data, see James H. Cassedy, *American Medicine and Statistical Thinking, 1800–1860* (New York: ToExcel, 1999); Dan Bouk, *How Our Days Became Numbered: Risk and the Rise of the Statistical Individual* (Chicago: University of Chicago Press, 2018); Colin Koopman, *How We Became Our Data: A Genealogy of the Informational Person* (Chicago: University of Chicago Press, 2019).

13. See Sonia Shah, *Fever: How Malaria Has Ruled Humankind for 500,000 Years* (New York: Picador, 2011); R. Allan Freeze and Jay H. Lehr, *The Fluoride Wars: How a Modest Public Health Measure Became America's Longest-Running Political Melodrama* (New York: Wiley, 2009); Elizabeth Etheridge, *The Butterfly Caste: A Social History of Pellagra* (Westport, CT: Greenwood, 1972); Bob H. Reinhardt, *The End of a Global Pox: America and the Eradication of Smallpox in the Cold War Era* (Chapel Hill: University of North Carolina Press, 2015).

14. *Daily Hampshire Gazette*, March 8, 1815. See also Drew Gilpin Faust, *Death and the American Civil War* (New York, Vintage, 2008).

15. "Casualty Notification Guide for the Casualty Notification Officer," Fort Lee Casualty Assistance Center, May 15, 2013, https://home.army.mil /lee/application/files/5815/3797/1469/CNO_GUIDE_2013.pdf.

16. "Preamble of the Charter of the United Nations," https://www.un.org /en/about-us/un-charter/preamble; accessed April 25, 2021.

17. "The State vs. the Body of the Slave, Polima," January 19, 1824, South Carolina Department of Archives and History; "The State vs. the Body of the Slave, Jeny," February 10, 1786, South Carolina Department of Archives and History; "The State vs. the Body of the Slave, Nelly," August 1, 1823, South Carolina Department of Archives and History, all at CSI: Dixie, https://csidixie.org/numbers/count-dead.

18. On the rise of for-profit life insurance, see Sharon Ann Murphy, *Investing in Life: Insurance in Antebellum America* (Baltimore: Johns Hopkins University Press, 2010); Viviana A. Rotman Zelzer, *Morals and Markets: The Development of Life Insurance in the United States* (New York: Columbia University Press, 2017).

## Chapter One

1. In the United States, the dip in mortality that coincided with robust economic growth is called "the antebellum puzzle." For more, see Michael R. Haines, Lee A. Craig, and Thomas Weiss, "The Short and the Dead: Nutrition, Mortality, and the 'Antebellum Puzzle' in the United States," *Journal of Economic History* 63, no. 2 (June 2003): 382–413; Matthias Zehetmayer, "The Continuation of the Antebellum Puzzle: Stature in the U.S., 1847–1894," *European Review of Economic History* 15, no. 2 (August 2011): 313–27; Dora L. Costa, "Height, Weight, and Disease among the Native-Born in the Rural, Antebellum North," *Social Science History* 17, no. 3 (Autumn 1993): 355–83. On the sharp rise in life expectancy in the United States, see Robert V. Wells, "The Mortality Transition in Schenectady, New York, 1880–1930," *Social Science History* 19, no. 3 (Autumn 1995): 399–423; Edward Meeker, "The Social Rate of Return on Investment in Public Health, 1880–1910," *Journal of Economic History* 34, no. 2 (June 1974): 392–421.

2. Alan Stedall, *Marcus Aurelius: The Dialogues* (self-pub., 2006), PublishDrive, 2; James Harvey Robinson, *Petrarch: The First Modern Scholar and Man of Letters* (New York: Haskell House, 1970), 130. There is some debate as to whether the Antonine plague was bubonic plague or smallpox. See also Kyle Harper, *The Fate of Rome: Climate, Disease, and the End of an Empire* (Princeton, NJ: Princeton University Press, 2019).

3. Tecumseh, "Sleep Not Longer, O Choctaws and Chickasaws" (speech), September 1811, in *Great Speeches by Native Americans*, ed. Bob Blaisdell (Mineola, NY: Dover, 2000), 50–51. See also Charles C. Mann, *1491: New Revelations of the Americas Before Columbus* (New York: Vintage, 2006); Sam White, *A Cold Welcome: The Little Ice Age and Europe's Encounter with Native Americans* (Cambridge, MA: Harvard University Press, 2020).

4. Elizabeth Gaskell, *The Life of Charlotte Brontë* (Edinburgh: John Grant, 1905), 46. *Life and Works of Charlotte Brontë and Her Sisters*, vol. 4, *The Professor, by Currer Bell. With Poems* (London: Smith, Elder, 1877), 447.

5. William Gilmore Simms to Edward Spann Hammond, November 20, 1864, in *The Simms Reader: Selections from the Writings of William Gilmore Simms*, ed. John Caldwell Guilds (Charlottesville: University Press of Virginia, 2001), 86.

6. Thomas Holley Chivers, quoted in Jeffrey Meyers, *Edgar Allan Poe: His Life and Legacy* (Cooper Square Press, 2000), 129. Balzac, Browning, Burns, Chekov, Chopin, Irving, and Keats all died of tuberculosis, causing a friend of Elizabeth Barrett Browning's to wonder: "What, if genius should be nothing but scrofula?" Elizabeth Barrett to Robert Browning, October 14,

1845, in *The Letters of Robert Browning and Elizabeth Barrett Barrett, 1845–1846* (London: Smith, Elder, 1899), 1:240. Puccini's *La Boheme* may not have debuted until 1896, but the characters it was based on lived in Paris in the Hungry Forties. Virginia Poe and the model for Mimi were diagnosed simultaneously and would die a year apart.

7. René and Jean Dubos, *The White Plague: Tuberculosis, Man, and Society* (New Brunswick, NJ: Rutgers University Press, 1987), 58–59.

8. Clark Lawlor, "Transatlantic Consumptions: Disease, Fame, and Literary Nationalisms in the Davidson Sisters, Southey, and Poe," *Studies in the Literary Imagination* 36, no. 2 (Fall 2003): 112.

9. Wilfred S. Dowden, ed., *The Journal of Thomas Moore*, vol. 3, *1826–1830* (Newark, NJ: University of Delaware Press, 1983), 1120.

10. *The Writings of Henry David Thoreau*, vol. 6, *Summer*, ed. H. G. O. Blake (Boston: Houghton Mifflin, 1884), 101; *The Writings of Henry David Thoreau*, vol. 8, *Journal*, ed. Bradford Torrey (Boston: Houghton Mifflin, 1906), 391. See also Thomas Dormandy, *The White Death: A History of Tuberculosis* (New York: New York University Press, 2001).

11. Charles Ferris Gettemy, *The Decennial Census of the Commonwealth, 1915*, pt. 3, *Nativity, Color or Race, Illiteracy, Political Condition, Ages, and Conjugal Condition* (Boston: Wright and Potter, 1918), 305.

12. *New Orleans Daily Picayune*, June 23, 1853 reported in "The Plague in the South-West: The Great Yellow Fever Epidemic in 1853," *De Bow's Review*, vol. 15 (1853), 598.

13. *New Orleans Daily Crescent*, July 6, 1853. See also *Report on the Epidemic Yellow Fever of 1853* (New Orleans: Sanitary Commission, 1854); Urmi Engineer Willoughby, *Yellow Fever, Race, and Ecology in Nineteenth-Century New Orleans* (Baton Rouge: Louisiana State University Press, 2017); and especially Henry M. McKiven Jr., "The Political Construction of a Natural Disaster: The Yellow Fever Epidemic of 1853," *Journal of American History* 94, no. 3 (December 2007): 734–42.

14. *New Orleans Daily Picayune*, June 23, 1853.

15. On the broader history of sanitation and public health, see John Duffy, *The Sanitarians: A History of American Public Health* (Urbana: University of Illinois Press, 1992); Dorothy Porter, *Health, Civilization, and the State: A History of Public Health from Ancient to Modern Times* (Oxfordshire: Routledge, 1999); George Rosen, *A History of Public Health* (Baltimore: Johns Hopkins University Press, 2015); Randall M. Packard, *A History of Global Health: Interventions into the Lives of Others Peoples* (Baltimore: Johns Hopkins University Press, 2015).

16. As James H. Cassedy notes in *American Medicine and Statistical Thinking, 1800–1860*: "Benjamin Rush chalked some of Philadelphia's

health improvements up to the decline of wigs, the increased use of the umbrella, and recent introduction of round hats; negative factors were the wearing of light dresses which exposed the upper arms. 'The frequency of consumptions from this cause,' he wrote, 'has given rise to a saying that "the nakedness of the women, is the clothing of the physician."'" Cassedy, *American Medicine and Statistical Thinking* (Cambridge, MA: Harvard University Press, 1984), 8. For more on Rush, see David Barton, *Benjamin Rush: Signer of the Declaration of Independence* (Aledo, TX: WallBuilder Press, 1999).

17. Alexis de Tocqueville, quoted in Patricia Cline Cohen, *A Calculating People: The Spread of Numeracy in Early America* (London: Routledge, 2016), 3; Charles Dickens, *American Notes for General Circulation* (London: Chapman & Hall, 1913), 202.

18. Joshua S. Billings, "Why a State Should Have a Proper System of Vital Statistics," *Seventh Biennial Report of the State Board of Health of Maryland* (Annapolis: James Young, 1888), 515.

19. Billings, "Why a State," 515. See also James H. Cassedy, *John Shaw Billings: Science and Medicine in the Gilded Age* (Bethesda, MD: Xlibris, 2009).

20. Lemuel Shattuck, *Memorials of the Descendants of William Shattuck, the Progenitor of the Families That Have Borne His Name* (Boston: Dutton and Wentworth, 1855), 382.

21. Shattuck, *Memorials of the Descendants of William Shattuck*, 382–83. On the importance of Shattuck to public health, see C.-E. A. Winslow, "The Message of Lemuel Shattuck for 1948," *American Journal of Public Health* 39, no. 2 (February 1949): 156–62; Walter F. Willcox, "Lemuel Shattuck, Statist, Founder of the American Statistical Association," *Journal of the American Statistical Association* 35, no. 209, pt. 2 (March 1940): 224–35.

22. Edwin Chadwick, "Life Assurances—Diminution of Sickness and Mortality," *Westminster Review* 9 (1828), 384–421. See also Roger Watson, *Edwin Chadwick, Poor Law and Public Health* (New York: Longman, 1965); Willis Rudy, "Lemuel Shattuck of Boston and His European Mentors," *New England Social Studies Bulletin* 31, no. 1, 45–47.

23. Lemuel Shattuck, *The Vital Statistics of Boston* (Philadelphia: Lea & Blanchard, 1841), 16. On the price children paid during industrialization in the United States, see Gretchen A. Condran and Harold R. Lentzner, "Early Death: Mortality among Young Children in New York, Chicago, and New Orleans," *Journal of Interdisciplinary History* 34, no. 3 (Winter 2004): 315–54.

24. Shattuck, *Vital Statistics of Boston*, 4.

25. Lemuel Shattuck, *Report of the Sanitary Commission of Massachusetts, 1850* (Cambridge, MA: Harvard University Press, 1948), 32.

26. Margo J. Anderson, *The American Census: A Social History* (New Haven, CT: Yale University Press, 1988); Andrew Whitby, *The Sum of the People: How the Census Has Shaped Nations, from the Ancient World to the Modern Era* (New York: Basic Books, 2020); Paul Schor, *Counting Americans: How the U.S. Census Classified the Nation* (New York: Oxford University Press, 2019).

27. On the important history of standards and standardization, see Stephen Mihm, "The Standards of the State: Weights, Measures, and Nation Making in the Early American Republic," in *State Formations: Global Histories and Cultures of Statehood*, ed. John Brooke and Julia Straus, (Cambridge: Cambridge University Press, 2018), 190–201.

28. See James H. Cassedy, "The Roots of American Sanitary Reform, 1843–47: Seven Letters from John H. Griscom to Lemuel Shattuck," *Journal of the History of Medicine and Allied Sciences* 30, no. 2 (April 1975): 136–47. Griscom submitted his report, "A Brief Review of the Sanitary Condition of the City," in 1842, noting that immigration was crowding families into toxic environments, including 7,196 people who were living in 1,459 dank cellars and 6,618 families whose "address" was a rear courtyard or lean-to. Only in 1901, sixty years after this report, did the city enact a tenement law with teeth. See also Robert W. de Forest, "A Brief History of the Housing Movement in America," *Annals of the American Academy of Political and Social Science* 51 (January 1914): 8–16. "Horse, foot, and raccoons" is an American comedic bastardization of "horse, foot, and dragoons"; it was typically used to describe a complete rout in every military department: horse (cavalry), foot (infantry), and dragoons (mounted infantry).

29. William Faulkner, *Big Woods: The Hunting Stories* (New York: Random House, 1955), 1–2; "Annual Report, Office of the California State Registrar," December 20, 1859, in *Journals of the Legislature of the State of California*, 2:117. In Californians defense, their version of the law required registrants to pay to be registered—something that Shattuck explicitly said was the worst kind of disincentive.

30. Henry David Thoreau, *Walden, Or Life in the Woods* (Boston: Ticknor and Fields, 1854), 10; *The Complete Works of Ralph Waldo Emerson*, vol. 5, *English Traits* (New York: Houghton Mifflin, 1903), 252. It is staggering how completely Emerson (inadvertently) predicted America's slide into a post-fact, post-truth, roll-your-own-reality culture: "To believe your own thought, to believe that what is true for you in your private heart, is true for all men,—that is genius." See Kurt Andersen, "How America Lost Its Mind," *Atlantic*, September 2017, www.theatlantic.com/magazine/archive/2017/09/how-america-lost-its-mind/534231.

31. Cassedy, *American Medicine and Statistical Thinking*, 200; Lemuel Shattuck, *Letter to the Secretary of State, on the Registration of Births, Marriages and Deaths, in Massachusetts* (Boston, 1846), 28.

32. Review of *A History of the Town of Concord, from Its Earliest Settlement, to 1832*, by Lemuel Shattuck, *North American Review* 42, no. 91 (April 1836): 451.

33. On the importance of the rise of the statistical profession for history more broadly, see David Salsburg, *The Lady Tasting Tea: How Statistics Revolutionized Science in the Twentieth Century* (New York: Holt, 2002).

34. See Anderson, *American Census*, 43–46.

35. Lemuel Shattuck, *Report to the Committee of the City Council Appointed to Obtain the Census of Boston for the Year 1845* (Boston: John H. Eastburn, 1846), iv.

36. David Outlaw to Emily Outlaw, January 29, 1849, David Outlaw Papers, Southern Historical Collection, University of North Carolina, Chapel Hill.

37. On improvements in the seventh census, see Opal G. Regan, "Statistical Reforms Accelerated by Sixth Census Error," *Journal of the American Statistical Association* 68, no. 343 (September 1973): 540–46. On the interstate slave trade, see Robert H. Gudmestad, *A Troublesome Commerce: The Transformation of the Interstate Slave Trade* (Baton Rouge: Louisiana State University Press, 2003); David L. Lightner, *Slavery and the Commerce Power: How the Struggle against the Interstate Slave Trade Led to the Civil War* (New Haven, CT: Yale University Press, 2006); Walter Johnson, *Soul by Soul: Life Inside the Antebellum Slave Market* (Cambridge, MA: Harvard University Press, 1999); Steven Deyle, *Carry Me Back: The Domestic Slave Trade in American Life* (Oxford: Oxford University Press, 2006).

38. Cong. Globe, 31st Cong., 1st Sess. 674 (1850).

39. Johnson Jones Hooper, *Adventures of Captain Simon Suggs, Late of the Tallapoosa Volunteers, Together with "Taking the Census" and Other Alabama Sketches* (Tuscaloosa: University of Alabama Press, 2015).

40. Ta-Nehisi Coates, *We Were Eight Years in Power: An American Tragedy* (New York: One World, 2017), 185.

41. J. D. B De Bow, *Mortality Statistics of the Seventh Census of the United States, 1850* (Washington, DC: A. G. P. Nicholson, 1855), 5.

42. De Bow, *Mortality Statistics*, 8.

43. Richard H. Steckel, "The Quality of Census Data for Historical Inquiry: A Research Agenda," *Social Science History* 15, no. 4 (Winter 1991): 579–99. On the historic development of shame around masturbation, see Thomas W. Laqueur, *Solitary Sex: A Cultural History of Masturbation* (Princeton, NJ: Zone Books, 2004).

44. Edward Jarvis to J. D. B. De Bow, September 22, 1855, reprinted in De Bow, *Mortality Statistics*, 45, 46.

45. De Bow, *Mortality Statistics*, 48, 9.

46. John Eberle, review of *The Influence of Tropical Climates on European Constitutions*, by James Johnson, *American Medical Recorder* 4, no. 3 (1821): 543, 542.

47. To explore the specific numbers and ratios uncovered in our datafication of the 1850 mortality census, see "Mortality Census Visualizations," accessed August 22, 2021, https://csidixie.org/numbers/mortality-census/visualizations.

48. On the high numbers of smothered among the enslaved population, revealed by the 1850 mortality census, see Michael T. Johnson, "Smother Slave Infants: Were Slave Mothers at Fault?," *Journal of Southern History* 47, no. 4 (November 1981): 493–520. The spatial distributions of deaths uncovered in the 1850 census can also be confirmed by later mortality censuses. In writing up the findings of the 1890 mortality census, John S. Billings noted that "deaths reported as due to gunshot wounds . . . were most frequent in the southwestern and southern states . . . and [were] comparatively few on the North and Middle Atlantic coast regions." He further noted that suicides were "relatively lowest in the South and higher in West and New England." *Report on Vital and Social Statistics in U.S. at 11th Census, 1890* (Washington, DC: Government Printing Office, 1896), xciv. For more on the effects of the gender imbalance during the gold rush, see Susan Lee Johnson, *Roaring Camp: The Social World of the California Gold Rush* (New York: W. W. Norton, 2000).

49. Charles-Edward Amory Winslow, *The Conquest of Epidemic Disease: A Chapter in the History of Ideas* (Madison: University of Wisconsin Press, 1980), v; Steven Johnson, *The Ghost Map: The Story of London's Most Terrifying Epidemic—and How It Changed Science, Cities, and the Modern World* (New York: Riverhead Books, 1987), 15. On the gradual improvement of the census, see J. David Hacker, "New Estimates of Census Coverage in the United States, 1850–1930," *Social Science History* 37, no. 1 (Spring 2013): 71–101. In his abstract to the article, Hacker notes, "The 1880 census appears to have achieved the most complete coverage of the native-born white population before 1940" (71). See also T. H. Hollingsworth, "The Importance of the Quality of the Data in Historical Demography," *Daedalus* 97, no. 2 (Spring 1968): 415–32.

50. Jean V. Berlin, *Sherman's Civil War: Selected Correspondence of William T. Sherman, 1860–1865* (Chapel Hill: University of North Carolina Press, 2014), 782.

51. See Judith Giesberg, "'A Muster Roll of the American People': The 1870 Census, Voting Rights, and the Postwar South," *Journal of Southern History* 87, no. 1 (February 2021): 35–66; Anderson, *American Census*.

52. Arthur L. Kellermann and Donald T. Reay, "Protection or Peril?" *New England Journal of Medicine* 314 (June 1986): 1557–60. See also Arthur Kellermann, Frederick P. Rivara, Norman B. Rushforth, et al., "Gun Ownership as a Risk Factor for Homicide in the Home," *New England Journal of Medicine* 329 (October 1993): 1084–91. For the "Dickey Amendment," see 104th Congress, Pub. L. No. 104–208, 110 Stat. 3009 (1996), www.govinfo .gov/content/pkg/PLAW-104publ208/pdf/PLAW-104publ208.pdf.

53. Amanda Marcotte, "Trump Doesn't Want Coronavirus Testing: His Instinct Is Always to Hide the Truth," *Salon*, April 22, 2020, www.salon.com /2020/04/22/trump-doesnt-want-coronavirus-testing-his-instinct-is-always -to-hide-the-truth. See also Maggie Koerth, "The Uncounted Dead: Why Some People Who Likely Died from COVID-19 Aren't Included in the Final Numbers," *FiveThirtyEight*, May 20, 2020.

54. Prabhat Jha, "Counting the Dead Is One of the World's Best Investments to Reduce Premature Mortality," *Hypothesis* 10, no. 1 (2012): 1.


*Chapter Two*

Note on epigraph source: In his farewell address to the cadets at West Point in May 1962, General Douglas MacArthur attributed this quotation to Plato. Ridley Scott followed MacArthur in presenting the quote at the beginning of *Black Hawk Down*. Whether MacArthur is the original source of the misattribution or was following someone else is unknown. Regardless, no Plato scholar has been able to find this quotation among his writings, but it definitely appears in George Santayana, *Soliloquies in England* (New York: Scribner's, 1924), 102.

1. See Stephen Berry, *All That Makes a Man: Love and Ambition in the Civil War South* (New York: Oxford University Press, 2003), 228.

2. *Harper's Weekly*, December 22, 1860, 802; Laurence Keitt to Susan Keitt, February 11, 1864, Lawrence Massillon Keitt Papers, David M. Rubenstein Rare Book & Manuscript Library, Duke University (hereafter Keitt Papers); Dr. Theodoric Pryor to Susan Keitt, June 17, 1864, Keitt Papers.

3. *This Infernal War: The Confederate Letters of Edwin H. Fay* (Austin: University of Texas Press, 1958), 51.

4. Kent Gramm, *Battle: The Nature and Consequences of Civil War Combat* (Tuscaloosa: University of Alabama Press, 2008); Ralph Waldo Emerson

to James Elliot Cabot, August 4, 1861, in *The Selected Letters of Ralph Waldo Emerson*, ed. Joel Myerson (Columbia University Press, 1999), 405–6.

5. See Edward Achorn, *Every Drop of Blood: The Momentous Second Inauguration of Abraham Lincoln* (New York: Atlantic Monthly Press, 2020); Ronald C. White Jr., *Lincoln's Greatest Speech: The Second Inaugural* (New York: Simon & Schuster, 2006).

6. Noah Brooks, reporter for the *Sacramento Union*, claimed to have heard Lincoln make this statement in an article he wrote after the assassination. See *Harper's Weekly*, July 1865.

7. Elizabeth Brown Pryor, *Clara Barton, Professional Angel* (Philadelphia: University of Pennsylvania Press, 2011), 140. More than 40 percent of all Union prisoners who died in captivity died at Andersonville. On Andersonville, see Ovid L. Futch, *History of Andersonville Prison* (Gainesville: University Press of Florida, 2011); Benjamin G. Cloyd, *Haunted by Atrocity: Civil War Prisons in American Memory* (Baton Rouge, Louisiana State University Press, 2016). For more on Clara Barton, see Stephen B. Oates, *A Woman of Valor: Clara Barton and the Civil War* (New York: Free Press, 1994). Walt Whitman also had Barton's capacity for seeing the war at multiple scales simultaneously. When his brother George was wounded at Fredericksburg, Whitman traveled to see him. George turned out to be fine, but Whitman was never the same. "[These] tens and twenties of thousands of American young men," he noted, "badly wounded, all sorts of wounds, operated on, pallid with diarrhea, languishing, dying with fever, pneumonia, open a new world somehow to me, giving closer insights, new things, exploring deeper mines than any yet, showing our humanity . . . tried by terrible, fearfulest tests, probed deepest, the living soul's, the body's tragedies, bursting the petty bounds of art." Walt Whitman to Nathaniel Bloom and John F. S. Gray, March 19 and 20, 1863, in *Selected Letters of Walt Whitman*, ed. Edwin Haviland Miller (Iowa City: University of Iowa Press, 1990), 52.

8. Dorence Atwater, *A List of the Union Soldiers Buried at Andersonville* (New York: Tribune Association, 1866). As a data project, Atwater's list is interesting not only for the long list of names but also for the long list of causes of death. Of the roughly thirteen thousand dead, more than a third died of diarrhea/dysentery. Scurvy (scorbutus) and wounds were also prevalent causes of death.

9. Thomas P. Lowry, *From Andersonville to Tahiti: The Dorence Atwater Story* (self-pub., 2008), BookSurge.

10. Quotes from Judith Giesberg, *Army at Home: Women and the Civil War on the Northern Homefront* (Chapel Hill: University of North Carolina

Press, 2012), 153. On soldiers inventing their own means of being identified postmortem, see Drew Gilpin Faust, *This Republic of Suffering: Death and the American Civil War* (New York: Vintage, 2008), 102–19.

11. "Brady's Photographs: The Dead of Antietam," *New York Times*, October 20, 1862. This section on casualty lists and Civil War literature is indebted to Vanessa Steinroetter, "'Reading the List': Casualty Lists and Civil War Poetry," *ESQ: A Journal of the American Renaissance* 59, no. 1 (2013): 48–78. Steinroetter generally agrees with Geoffrey C. Bowker and Susan Leigh Star, who see "lists, especially standardized, official lists as important steps in the consolidation of national power and control." As they put it, the "material culture of bureaucracy and empire is not found in pomp and circumstance, nor even in the first instance at the point of a gun, but rather at the point of a list." Bowker and Star, *Sorting Things Out: Classification and Its Consequences* (Cambridge, MA: MIT Press, 1999). In this interpretive schema, these casualty lists, while not created by the state, are essentially modern in their tendency to buff out a man's rough edges and reduce him to a data point; he's just another man who gave his life for the state. Certainly I agree and have argued in this very book that data conception and data projection are keys to state power. In very different ways, however, Steinroetter and I both argue that casualty lists also pull in other directions. Steinroetter insists we pay attention to how these lists were "consumed" as literature. "Lists *can* be a way of sanitizing and simplifying knowledge," she notes, but they can also "be seen as more than mere displays of data when the reader looks for the human experience and stories hidden behind numbers and names (175)." In my argument, you don't even have to get *behind* the numbers and names to understand a list's power to push back against the state. Yes, a list can reduce and enslave—the manifest of a slave ship, for instance. But in the right hands, a list can be a democratic instrument, demanding that everyone be treated the same or accounted for or acknowledged. Indeed, the list, as I have argued here, is one of the few data representations that can convey enormity without sacrificing individuality. For other divergent and compelling interpretations of lists, see Alison Adam, "List," in *Software Studies: A Lexicon*, ed. Matthew Fuller (Cambridge, MA: MIT Press, 2008); Robert E. Belknap, *The List: The Uses and Pleasures of Cataloguing* (New Haven, CT: Yale University Press, 2004).

12. Joshua Foer, *Moonwalking with Einstein: The Art and Science of Remembering Everything* (New York: Penguin, 2012).

13. Andrej Petrovic, "Casualty Lists in Performance: Name Catalogues and Greek Verse-Inscriptions," in *Dialect, Diction, and Style in Greek Literary and Inscribed Epigram*, ed. Evina Sistakou and Anontios Rengakos (Walter

de Gruyter, 2016), 366. He calls the casualty list not a thing but "a culture of commemoration capable of *storing, preserving* and *transmitting* a significant amount of (metrically and mnemonically uncomfortable) data" (364).

14. Herman Melville, *Battle-Pieces and Aspects of the War* (Harper & Brothers, 1866), 253–54.

15. Thomas J. Brown, *Civil War Monuments and the Militarization of America* (Chapel Hill: University of North Carolina Press, 2019), 27, 55.

16. Brown, *Civil War Monuments*, 64.

17. J. T. Trowbridge, *The South: A Tour of Its Battle-Fields and Ruined Cities* (Hartford, CT: L. Stebbins, 1866), iii. Note: Portions of this material on Gettysburg were previously published in altered form as Stephen Berry, "Casualties of War: The Dead of Gettysburg," *Civil War Monitor* (July 2013). Permission has been given by the publisher to repurpose.

18. Trowbridge, *The South*, 17.

19. Trowbridge, *The South*, 19–20.

20. Trowbridge, *The South*, 17. See Garry Wills, *Lincoln at Gettysburg: The Words That Remade America* (New York: Simon & Schuster, 1992).

21. On the death of Isaac Taylor, see Travis W. Busey and John W. Busey, *Union Casualties at Gettysburg: A Comprehensive Record* (Jefferson, NC: McFarland, 2011), 316. On the death of Alfred Sofield, see Jeffrey J. Kowalis and Loree L. Kowalis, *Died at Gettysburg!* (Highstown, NJ: Longstreet House, 1998), 220. On the death of Travis Maxey, see Warren Wilkinson and Steven E. Woodworth, *Scythe of Fire: Through the Civil War with One of Lee's Most Legendary Regiments* (New York: HarperCollins, 2002), 237.

22. On the death of Samuel Zook, see Kowalis and Kowalis, *Died at Gettysburg!*, 15–21. On the death of James McCleary, see Gregory A. Coco, *Killed in Action: Eyewitness Accounts of the Last Moments of 100 Union Soldiers Who Died at Gettysburg* (Gettysburg, PA: Thomas, 1992), 55 (hereafter cited as *KIAU*). On the death of John Cranston, see Busey and Busey, *Union Casualties at Gettysburg*, 519. On the death of Robert Crawford, see Gregory A. Coco, *Confederates Killed in Action at Gettysburg* (Gettysburg, PA: Thomas, 2001), 90 (hereafter cited as *KIAC*).

23. The lieutenant who questioned his superior—"Well, it is murder, but it is the order"—was Charles R. Mudge of the Second Massachusetts. Kowalis and Kowalis, *Died at Gettysburg!*, 35. "Oh God! I am shot" were the final words of Second Lieutenant Silas A. Miller, Co. A, Twelfth U.S. Infantry. As one witness noted: "I think your brother must have been hit, about 6 P.M. He was shot through the body, near the heart.—said, Oh! God, I am shot.—was moved to a rock near, and only lived about ten minutes, he spoke no more, was unable, & evidently expected death." *KIAU*, 73. "I am killed"

were the last words of Private James Johnston, Co. K, Fourth Michigan. As a witness recalled, "My tent mate James Johnston was shot He was but a fiew feet in front of me when He fell. I herd Him Say I am Killed this was the last words that I herd Him speak the rest was groans there was no help for Him." *KIAU*, 44. "Who shall care for Mother now?" were the final words of Private William Purbeck, Fifth Massachusetts Light Artillery. As Corporal Benjamin Graham recalled, "When little Purbeck, a good, smart boy, only 17, saw the man and horse down, and started to over towards them, when he, too, got hit in the side with a piece of shell. He was taken to the rear and to the hospital, where he died that night, and as he was dying he uttered these words,—'Who will care for Mother now?'" *KIAU*, 50.

24. On the death of Samuel Spear, see *KIAU*, 69. On the death of Sumner Paine, see Busey and Busey, *Union Casualties at Gettysburg*, 209. On the death of Jonathan Leavitt, see *KIAU*, 79–80.

25. On the death of Charles Taylor, see *KIAU*, 58–59.

26. "Proceedings of Coroner's Inquest into the Death of J. H. Chapin, Killed June 9, 1893, in the Fall of the Building Known as Ford's Theater," Records of the Joint Committees of Congress, RG 128, National Archives.

27. Abraham Lincoln, "Second State of the Union Address," December 1, 1862, National Archives, www.archives.gov/legislative/features/sotu/lincoln.html; Shelby Foote, *The Civil War: A Narrative*. See also Edmund Wilson, *Patriotic Gore: Studies in the Literature of the American Civil War* (London: Deutsch, 1962).

28. "United Nations Charter: Preamble," https://www.un.org/en/about-us/un-charter/preamble.

29. See Robert W. Doubek, *Creating the Vietnam Veterans Memorial: The Inside Story* (Jefferson, NC: McFarland, 2015).

30. Maya Lin, "Making the Memorial," *New York Review of Books*, November 2, 2000. The National Memorial for Peace and Justice in Montgomery, Alabama, uses a different technique to achieve the same effect of conveying simultaneously the twin scales of human catastrophe. In the forest of suspended coffins, a visitor experiences some sense of the scale of the disaster while never losing sight of the individual names inscribed on the oxidized steel. In his review of the installation, Philip Kennicott, art and architecture critic for the *Washington Post*, compared the memorial to an "open air morgue." See Philip Kennicott, "A Powerful Memorial in Montgomery Remembers the Victims of Lynching," *Washington Post*, April 24, 2018.

31. Drew Gilpin Faust, "'We Should Grow Too Fond of It': Why We Love the Civil War" *Civil War History* 50, no. 4 (December 2004): 23.

32. Elisabeth Bumiller, "U.S. Lifts Photo Ban on Military Coffins," *New York Times*, December 7, 2009, www.nytimes.com/2009/02/27/world /americas/27iht-photos.1.20479953.html; Scott L. Althaus, Nathaniel Swigger, Svitlana Chernykh, David J. Hendry, Sergio C. Wals, and Christopher Tiwald, "Uplifting Manhood to Wonderful Heights? News Coverage of the Human Costs of Military Conflict from World War I to Gulf War Two," *Political Communication* 31, no. 2 (2014): 201.

33. Faust, "'We Should Grow Too Fond of It,'" 377, 382.

## Chapter Three

1. "Hard to Please," *Athens Southern Watchman*, March 20, 1867, 3. "Homicide," *Athens Southern Watchman*, March 13, 1867, 3. See also Richard H. Steckel, "A Dreadful Childhood: The Excess Mortality of American Slaves," *Social Science History* 10, no. 4 (Winter 1986): 427–65.

2. "Homicide," *Athens Southern Watchman*, 3; "Hard to Please," *Athens Southern Watchman*, 3.

3. While this chapter focuses on the murdered Black dead, the massive racial disparity in human health outcomes is apparent throughout the American historical record. See, for instance, Charles S. Sydnor, "Life Span of Mississippi Slaves," *American Historical Review* 35, no. 3 (April 1930): 566–73; Richard H. Steckel, "Slave Mortality: Analysis of Evidence from Plantation Records," *Social Science History* 3, no. 3/4 (1979): 86–114; Christian Warren, "Northern Chills, Southern Fevers: Race-Specific Mortality in American Cities, 1730–1900," *Journal of Southern History* 63, no. 1 (April 1997): 23–56; Werner Troesken, "The Limits of Jim Crow: Race and the Provision of Water and Sewerage Services in American Cities, 1880–1925," *Journal of Economic History* 62, no. 3 (September 2002): 734–72.

4. See Sven Beckert and Seth Rockman, eds., *Slavery's Capitalism: A New History of American Economic Development* (Philadelphia: University of Pennsylvania Press, 2016), especially the first chapter, "Slavery's Technology," in which Ed Baptist explores the source of the "astounding productivity improvements" (14) on antebellum cotton plantations. Eli Whitney's cotton gin, new land, and new varietals certainly had something to do with it, but Baptist finds the main source elsewhere—in the systematic use of violence. Between 1790 and 1860, planters created a "pushing system," a combination of increased surveillance, decreased breaks, lockstep labor, and, above all, an ever-rising quota system in which each hand had a number of pounds to bring in by the end of each day, with all shortfalls taken out on their backs. "The whip made cotton," Baptist concludes. "And whip-made increases in

the efficiency of picking had global significance" (52). This may seem too brutal to be "modern" and too simple to be sophisticated, but Baptist makes a convincing case that it was the beginning of scientific management. At the same time, one can't help but feel that by strongly associating slavery with capitalism, the purpose is to indict capitalism as much as slavery.

5. Quoted in Mark V. Tushnet, *Slave Law in the American South: State v. Mann in History and Literature* (Lawrence: University Press of Kansas, 2003), 1–2. As Tushnet notes, Harriet Beecher Stowe paid significant attention to Ruffin's decision in both her *Key to Uncle Tom's Cabin* and her second antislavery novel, *Dred: A Tale of the Great Dismal Swamp.* The intention of her work, she always said, was "to separate carefully, as far as possible, the system from the men" (2). There were good men in the South, Stowe said, and Thomas Ruffin was obviously one of them. But the institution of slavery corrupted the minds and morals of all who sought to defend it.

6. Thomas Reade Rootes Cobb, *An Inquiry into the Law of Negro Slavery in the United States of America* (Philadelphia: T. & J. W. Johnson, 1858): 91, 95, 90, 93. See also Thomas A. Foster, *Rethinking Rufus: Sexual Violations of Enslaved Men* (Athens: University of Georgia Press, 2019); Andrew T. Fede, *Homicide Justified: The Legality of Killing Slaves in the United States and the Atlantic World* (Athens: University of Georgia Press, 2017).

7. Hiram Fuller, *Belle Brittan on a Tour, at Newport, and Here and There* (New York: Derby & Jackson, 1858), 112.

8. R. F. Hunnisett, *The Medieval Coroner* (Cambridge: Cambridge University Press, 1961).

9. Shakespeare, *Hamlet*, act 5, scene 1.

10. "An Act Concerning the Office, Duties and Liabilities of Coroner" (1839) in *Acts and Resolutions of the State of South Carolina* (D. & J.J. Faust, 1839), 74.

11. Laura F. Edwards, *A People and Their Peace: Legal Culture and the Transformation of Inequality in the Post-Revolutionary South* (Chapel Hill: University of North Carolina Press, 2009). The history of death investigation in America deserves far more attention. See Jeffrey M. Jentzen, *Death Investigation in America: Coroners, Medical Examiners, and the Pursuit of Medical Certainty* (Cambridge, MA: Harvard University Press, 2009). For the history of death in the American South more broadly, see Craig Thompson Friend and Lorri Glover, eds., *Death and the American South* (Cambridge, MA: Cambridge University Press, 2014).

12. "The State vs. the Dead Body of Edward," August 3, 1824, South Carolina Department of Archives and History, https://csidixie.org/inquests/2684. The following paragraphs draw on testimony from this document.

13. "The State vs. the Dead Body of Ellick," April 26, 1851, South Carolina Department of Archives and History, https://csidixie.org/inquests/3445.

14. "State vs. the Dead Body of Ellick."

15. "The State vs. the Dead Body of Peter," June 16, 1838, South Carolina Department of Archives and History, https://csidixie.org/inquests/2352; "The State vs. the Dead Body of Randal," May 9, 1844, South Carolina Department of Archives and History, https://csidixie.org/inquests/2350.

16. Abraham Lincoln, "Annual Message to Congress," December 1, 1862, in Roy P. Basler, *Collected Works of Abraham Lincoln* (New Brunswick, NJ: Rutgers University Press, 1953), 5:537.

17. Norman R. Yetman, ed., *Voices from Slavery: 100 Authentic Slave Narratives* (Courier Corporation, 2021), 132; *The Frederick Douglass Papers*, ser. 2, vol. 3 (New Haven, CT: Yale University Press, 2012), 54.

18. The study of the Slave Power's commitment to disciplining poor whites starts with Keri Leigh Merritt, *Masterless Men: Poor Whites and Slavery in the Antebellum South* (Cambridge: Cambridge University Press, 2017). See also Jeff Forret, *Race Relations at the Margins: Slaves and Poor Whites in the Antebellum Countryside* (Baton Rouge: Louisiana State University Press, 2010); Luther Adams, "Tipling [*sic*] toward Freedom: Alcohol and Emancipation," *Register of the Kentucky Historical Society* 117, no. 2 (Spring 2019): 323–43.

19. Lynn Hunt, *Inventing Human Rights: A History* (New York: W. W. Norton, 2007).

20. Elizabeth L. Norris to Emilie Todd Helm, September 28, 1895, Elizabeth L. Norris Collection, Abraham Lincoln Presidential Library & Museum.

21. Elizabeth B. Clark, "'The Sacred Rights of the Weak': Pain, Sympathy, and the Culture of Individual Rights in Antebellum America," *Journal of American History* 82, no. 2 (September 1995): 480; Jonathan Edwards, *The Works of President Edwards*, vol. 6 (New York: Burt Franklin, 1817), 458; G. Frederick Wright, *Charles Grandison Finney* (Boston: Houghton, Mifflin, 1891), 100.

22. *American Slavery as It Is: Testimony of a Thousand Witnesses* (New York: American Anti-Slavery Society, 1839); Theodore Dwight Weld to Gerritt Smith, October 23, 1839, in *Letters of Theodore Dwight Weld and Angelina Grimké Weld and Sarah Grimké, 1822–1844* (Gloucester, MA: Peter Smith, 1965), 807.

23. *American Slavery as It Is*, 77.

24. Ellen Gruber Garvey, "Nineteenth-Century Abolitionists and the Databases They Created," *Legacy* 27, no. 2 (2010): 359; Angelina

Grimké Weld to Anna R. Frost, quoted in Garvey, "Nineteenth-Century Abolitionists," 365. The impulse of the Black community to create a record that might sponsor a reckoning has a long history. I am thinking particularly of W. E. B. Du Bois's work at *The Crisis*, especially "The Waco Horror," *The Crisis*, July 1916. See also W. E. B. *Du Bois's Data Portraits: Visualizing Black America* (Princeton, NJ: Princeton Architectural Press, 2018).

25. Eric Foner, *Reconstruction: America's Unfinished Revolution, 1863–1877* (New York: Harper & Row, 1988); Leon Litwack, *Been in the Storm So Long: The Aftermath of Slavery* (New York: Vintage, 1980); Steven Hahn, *A Nation under Our Feet: Black Political Struggles in the Rural South from Slavery to the Great Migration* (Cambridge, MA: Belknap Press of Harvard University Press, 2003); David W. Blight, *Race and Reunion: The Civil War in American Memory* (Cambridge, MA: Belknap Press of Harvard University Press, 2001); Gregory P. Downs, *After Appomattox: Military Occupation and the Ends of War* (Cambridge, MA: Harvard University Press, 2019). On Rivers's attempt to find justice in the breech, see Stephen Berry, "The Hamburg Massacre," CSI: Dixie, accessed August 22, 2021, https://csidixie.org/chronicles/hamburg-massacre; Stephen Budiansky, *The Bloody Shirt: Terror after the Civil War* (New York: Penguin Books, 2008), 219–54.

26. See "'Murders and Outrages' in South Carolina, 1866–1868," CSI: Dixie, accessed August 22, 2021, https://csidixie.org/exodus/coroners-freedmen.

27. William A. Blair, *The Record of Murders and Outrages: Racial Violence and the Fight over Truth at the Dawn of Reconstruction* (Chapel Hill: University of North Carolina Press, 2021).

28. "The State vs. the Dead Body of S. G. W. Dill, Nestor Ellison," June 5, 1868, South Carolina Department of Archives and History, https://csidixie.org/inquests/2847.

29. "State vs. the Dead Body of S. G. W. Dill."

30. Kay Wright Lewis, *A Curse upon the Nation: Race Freedom, and Extermination in American and the Atlantic World* (Athens: University of Georgia Press, 2017).

31. "State vs. the Dead Body of S. G. W. Dill"; George F. Price, First Lieutenant, Fifth U.S. Cavalry, to Louis V. Caziarc, Assistant Adjutant General, June 22, 1868, in *Annual Report of the Secretary of War*, vol. 1 (Washington, DC: Government Printing Office, 1868), 471.

32. *The United States Army and Navy Journal and Gazette*, vol. 25 (September 17, 1887), 139.

33. George Frederic Price, *Across the Continent with the Fifth Cavalry* (New York: D. Van Nostrand, 1883), 128.

34. Price to Caziarc, June 22, 1868, 470, 472.

35. Price to Caziarc, June 22, 1868, 472–73.

36. Price to Caziarc, June 22, 1868, 473; Price, *Across the Continent*, 129. Price's frustration with the South's "pleasant people" is eerily echoed by Martin Luther King, who identified the "white moderate" as the main enemy in his "Letter from a Birmingham Jail." "Shallow understanding from people of goodwill," he noted, "is more frustrating than absolute misunderstanding from people of ill will. Lukewarm acceptance is much more bewildering than outright rejection." See Jonathan Rieder, *Gospel of Freedom: Martin Luther King, Jr.'s "Letter from Birmingham Jail" and the Struggle That Changed a Nation* (New York: Bloomsbury Press, 2013).

37. Amy J. Ross, "The Body Counts: Civilian Casualties and the Crisis of Human Rights," in *Human Rights in Crisis*, ed. Alice Bullard (Burlington, VT: Ashgate, 2008), 35–47; Human Rights Data Analysis Group, "About Us," accessed August 2, 2019, https://hrdag.org/aboutus.

38. Historians debate whether Stalin said this line or anything like it. Mary Soames (daughter of Churchill) claimed she overheard the line, but other scholars attribute the idea to Erich Maria Remarque or Adolf Eichmann. For Spock quote, see *Star Trek: The Original Series*, season 2, episode 18, "The Immunity Syndrome," directed by Joseph Prevney, written by Robert Sabaroff, aired January 19, 1968. On "psychic numbing," see Paul Slovic, David Zionts, Andrew K. Woods, Ryan Goodman, and Derek Jinks, "Psychic Numbing and Mass Atrocities," in *Psychic Numbing and Mass Atrocities*, ed. E. Shafir (Princeton, NJ: Princeton University Press, 2013), 126–42.

39. Quoted in Peter J. DiDomenica and Thomas G. Robbins, *Journey from Genesis to Genocide: Hate, Empathy, and the Plight of Humanity* (Pittsburgh: Dorrance, 2013), 179. The history of the bystander effect begins with John M. Darley and Bibb Latane, "Bystander Intervention in Emergencies: Diffusion of Responsibility," *Journal of Personality and Social Psychology* 8, no. 4 (April 1968): 377–83. For a modification of the theory, suggesting that "in the presence of other bystanders, personal distress is [actually] enhanced, and fixed action patterns of avoidance and freezing dominate," see Ruud Hortensius and Beatrice de Gelder, "From Empathy to Apathy: The Bystander Effect Revisited," *Current Directions in Psychological Science* 27, no. 4 (August 2018): 249.

40. Vera Bergengruen, "'We Continue to Spin in Circles': Inside the Decades-Long Effort to Create a National Police Use-of-Force Database," *Time*, June 30, 2020, https://time.com/5861953/police-reform-use-of-force -database.

41. Bryan Schatz and Allie Gross, "Congress Is Finally Going to Make Local Law Enforcement Report How Many People They Kill," *Mother Jones*, December 17, 2014, www.motherjones.com/politics/2014/12/death-custody -reporting-act-police-shootings-ferguson-garner.

42. Al Baker, "Bias Seen in 'Police-on-Police' Shootings," *New York Times*, May 27, 2010. www.nytimes.com/2010/05/27/nyregion/27shoot.html.

## Epilogue

1. Scientists debate whether certain creatures, like the hydra, are biologically immortal because they do not undergo senescence. Like any creature, however, the hydra can be killed, so it is not immortal in that sense.

2. See especially Thomas W. Laqueur, *The Work of the Dead: A Cultural History of Mortal Remains* (Princeton, NJ: Princeton University Press, 2018); Allan Kellehear, *A Social History of Dying* (Cambridge: Cambridge University Press, 2007); Peter Metcalf and Richard Huntington, *Celebrations of Death: The Antropology of Mortuary Ritual* (Cambridge: Cambridge University Press, 1992); Maurice Bloch and Jonathan Parry, eds., *Death and the Regeneration of Life* (Cambridge: Cambridge University Press, 1982).

3. Andre Gide, *The Immoralist* (New York: Vintage, 1996), 68.

4. Voltaire, "Premiere Lettre sur Oedipe," in *Works*, vol. 1, 1785; for a detailed history of the context and evolution of Jefferson's comment, see "Madison on 'The Earth Belongs to the Living,'" in *The Papers of Thomas Jefferson*, ed. Julian P. Boyd, vol. 16, *November 1789 to July 1790* (Princeton, NJ: Princeton University Press, 1961), 146–66. See also Paul K. Saint-Amour, "The Reign of the Dead: Hauntologies of Postmortem Copyright," in *The Copywrights: Intellectual Property and the Literary Imagination* (New York: Cornell University Press, 2003). On the changing of Western death ways, see John McManners, *Death and the Enlightenment: Changing Attitudes to Death among Christians and Unbelievers in Eighteenth-Century France* (New York: Oxford University Press, 1981).

5. John Keats to Richard Woodhouse, October 27, 1818, in *Letters of John Keats to His Family and Friends*, ed. Sidney Colvin (London: MacMillan, 1891), 185.

6. Fustel de Coulanges quoted in Trygve R. Tholfsen, *Historical Thinking: An Introduction* (New York: Harper & Row, 1969), 201; Lord Acton, *A Lecture on the Study of History, Delivered at Cambridge, June 11, 1895* (London: Macmillan, 1895), 10.

7. Frederick Goldin, trans., *The Song of Roland* (New York: W. W. Norton, 1978), 14–18.

8. Jacques Derrida, *Archive Fever: A Freudian Impression* (Chicago: University of Chicago Press, 1998), 91; Carolyn Steedman, *Dust: The Archive and Cultural History* (New Brunswick, NJ: Rutgers University Press, 2002).

9. Ann Laura Stoler, "Colonial Archives and the Arts of Governance," *Archival Science* 2 (March 2002): 87.

10. Seminal volumes in the history of history itself include Julius Hare and Augustus William Hare, *Guesses at Truth, by Two Brothers* (London: James Duncan, 1827); March Bloch, *The Historian's Craft: Reflections on the Nature and Uses of History and the Techniques and Methods of Those Who Write It*, trans. Peter Putnam (New York: Vintage, 1964); Edward Hallet Carr, *What Is History?* (New York: Vintage, 1967); Jacques Barzun, *Clio and the Doctors: Psycho-History, Quanto-History and History* (Chicago: University of Chicago Press, 1974); Michel-Rolph Trouillot, *Silencing the Past: Power and the Production of History* (Boston: Beacon Press, 1995); Peter Novick, *That Noble Dream: The "Objectivity Question" and the American Historical Profession* (Cambridge: Cambridge University Press, 1988); John Lewis Gaddis, *The Landscape of History: How Historians Map the Past* (New York: Oxford University Press, 2004).

11. Emma Willard, *An Address to the Public: Particularly the Members of the Legislature of New York, Proposing a Plan for Improving Female Education* (Middlebury, VT: J. W. Copeland, 1819), 15; Emma Willard, *Willard's Historic Guide: Guide to the Temple of Time; and Universal History for Schools* (New York: A. S. Barnes, 1849), 14.

12. The story of niacin is a fascinating one. Technically known as nicotinic acid and more familiarly as vitamin $B_3$, niacin is an essential human nutrient. Without it we develop pellagra, which causes sensitivity to sunlight, dermatitis, diarrhea, hair loss, and ultimately trouble sleeping, weakness, dementia, and finally death. Native Americans rarely developed pellagra because of the way they processed corn, which they tended to soak in limewater and then boil before drying and crushing. This ensured that they were getting the full nutritional value of the corn, including the germ, which contains most of the niacin. With the rise of cotton monoculture in the post–Civil War South, Southerners devoted less acreage to food and became increasingly dependent on corn meal imported from the North. To create a shelf-stable product, Northern millers removed the oily germ, thereby removing much of its nutritional value, including the niacin. As a result, by 1928, pellagra had become epidemic in the South. When the boll weevil decimated cotton monoculture, agriculture diversified and the epidemic abated, but pellagra remained a problem until government policies began fortifying (enriching) flour with niacin and other vitamins. See Kumaravel

Rajakumar, "Pellagra in the United States: A Historical Perspective," *Southern Medical Journal* 93, no. 3 (March 2000): 272–77; A. J. Bollet, "Politics and Pellagra: The Epidemic of Pellagra in the U.S. in the Early Twentieth Century," *Yale Journal of Biology and Medicine* 65, no. 3 (May–June 1992): 211–21; Youngmee K. Park, Christopher T. Sempos, Curtis N. Barton, John E. Vanderveen, and Elizabeth A. Yetley, "Effectiveness of Food Fortification in the United States: The Case of Pellagra," *American Journal of Public Health* 90, no. 5 (May 2000): 727–38; Russell M. Wilder, "A Brief History of the Enrichment of Flour and Bread," *Journal of the American Medical Association* 162, no. 17 (1956): 1539–41.

# INDEX

Paine, Sumner, 49
Parker, Emanuel (murderer), 75
Peter (enslaved, murdered), 67
Petrarcha, Francesco, 2
Poe, Edgar Allan, 4, 7
Poe, Virginia, 4
*Preston* (blockade runner), 33–34
Price, Frederic, 77–79
public health, history of, 6–7

quantification, history of: ix–x.
    *See also* data

Randal (enslaved, murdered), 67
Rabon, Abraham (murderer), 75
Rivers, Joshua, 72
Rivers, Prince, 72
Rousseau, Jean-Jacques, 69
Ruffin, Edwin, 35
Ruffin, Thomas, 58–59
Rush, Benjamin, 7

Seward, William (U.S. Senator), 21
Shattuck, Lemuel: early life of, 9–11;
    death registration and, 8, 11–17;
    census and, 17–18
Sherman, William Tecumseh, 28
Simonides, 43
Simms, William Gilmore, 4
Snow, John, xi
Sofield, Alfred, 48
Spear, Samuel, 49
*State v. Mann*, 58–59
statistics, history of, xii

Stowe, Harriet Beecher, 72
Szent-Gyorgyi, Albert, 81

tally sticks, x
Taylor, Bayard, 50
Taylor, Charles Frederick, 49–50
Taylor, Isaac, 48
Taylor, Patrick 48
Tecumseh, 2
*Temple of Time*, 89–91
Thoreau, Henry David, 5
Tilman, Ben, 73
Troutman, Charles E., 50–51
Trowbridge, John, 46–47
Trump, Donald J., 31
tuberculosis, history of, 4–5
Tuggle, William (murderer), xvii

Uniform Crime Reporting, 82–83

vitamin deficiency, history of, 26

Watkins, Caleb (murderer), 67
Weld, Theodore, 70–71
worms (hookworm, whipworm, etc.),
    27
Willard, Emma, 89–90
Winslow, Charles-Edward, 28
Wright, Elizur, xi

yellow fever, in New Orleans, 1853,
    5–7

Zook, Samuel, 48

9 781469 667522